COLOSSUS

First US edition 2021
First published by Templar Books, an imprint of Bonnier Books UK, 2019

Library of Congress Catalog Card Number pending
ISBN 978-1-5362-1706-3

21 22 23 24 25 26 TLF 10 9 8 7 6 5 4 3 2 1

Printed in Dongguan, Guangdong, China

This book was typeset in Helvetica Neue and Ostrich Sans.
The illustrations were created digitally.

BIG PICTURE PRESS
an imprint of
Candlewick Press
99 Dover Street
Somerville, Massachusetts 02144

www.candlewick.com

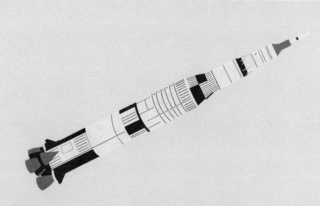

COLOSSUS

THE WORLD'S MOST AMAZING FEATS OF ENGINEERING

COLIN HYNSON

ILLUSTRATED BY GIULIA LOMBARDO

B P P

CONTENTS

ENGINEERS HAVE
GIVEN US HOUSING,
CREATED ENERGY, BUILT
ICONIC MONUMENTS,
AND EVEN SENT PEOPLE
INTO SPACE.

WHAT IS AN ENGINEER?

Everywhere you look, you can find incredible examples of engineering. Buildings, bridges, cars, even the pavement beneath your feet—these things have all been designed by engineers. But what exactly is an engineer?

To put it simply, an engineer is someone who finds practical solutions to everyday problems, often by utilizing math and physics. Thousands of years ago, early engineers designed bridges so travelers could cross obstacles safely. Over the centuries, innovative men and women have developed solutions to many of the challenges that humanity has faced—whether building houses to protect people from the elements or city walls to defend communities from attackers.

Some of the most extraordinary works of engineering were built to impress or as symbols of power or religion. In ancient civilizations, many structures were designed to honor gods or to commemorate powerful people. There are even famous structures that have been around for so long that we no longer know how or why they were built.

Today, engineers face new challenges. As the world's population expands, they need to find ways to build homes that use less space. Towering skyscrapers offer one solution, and some countries are even creating new islands in the sea. Innovative ways of producing energy are also being developed to combat climate change caused by the burning of fossil fuels.

Colossus explores some of the most innovative engineering in human history. From the pyramids of ancient Egypt to the world's tallest skyscraper, discover remarkable bridges and statues, continent-spanning railway lines, enormous space stations, and more—all brought to you by incredible engineers.

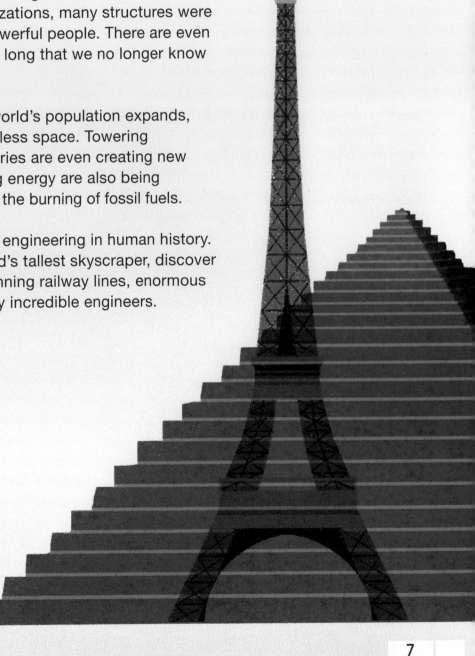

ANCIENT TECHNIQUES

Even today, we marvel at the size and ambition of many ancient structures. From the fortress city of Great Zimbabwe in Africa and the towering pyramids of Central America to the phenomenal Great Wall of China, our world is full of incredible feats of engineering. These massive structures are particularly impressive because they were designed and built without the benefit of the modern technology that we often take for granted.

AN ANCIENT STONE TEMPLE DISCOVERED IN TURKEY IS ALMOST 11,000 YEARS OLD—AND STILL STANDING.

THE GREAT PYRAMID OF GIZA

Giza, Egypt

At 482 feet/147 meters high, this 4,500-year-old pyramid was the world's tallest structure for about 3,800 years. Although nobody knows for sure how Egypt's pyramids were built, we do know that around 4,000 skilled laborers worked year-round for 20 years, alongside tens of thousands of enslaved people and unskilled workers. Paintings from the time show workers dragging heavy blocks of stone up ramps, but it is unclear how they were lifted into place. As the pyramid rose upward, the ramp needed to be made higher and longer.

Over 130 pyramids have been discovered in Egypt. Most were built as extravagant tombs for pharaohs.

The Great Pyramid is made of over 2 million blocks of limestone, each weighing 2.5 tons/2.3 metric tons.

HUMAN AND MACHINE POWER

Today, powerful machines are used to build huge structures, yet ancient civilizations had to do the same work using just the strength of humans and animals. It is estimated that over 100,000 workers built the Colosseum in ancient Rome, but the Empire State Building, 2,000 years later, was built by only 3,000 workers.

Modern tools also make building jobs much easier. In ancient civilizations, tools were much simpler and were usually made from local materials. The Mayan people in Central America built their enormous stone temples and palaces without any metal tools. Instead, they used a hard stone like flint or obsidian to work the softer stone of the buildings.

BUILDING MATERIALS

The glass, steel, and aluminum used to build the world's tallest modern skyscrapers come from all over the world.

Ancient civilizations could only rely on materials found nearby. The Great Wall of China (pages 42–43) was built over hundreds of years, starting in the seventh century BCE, and stretches for hundreds of miles. It is made of stone in some places and bricks and soil in others. This all depended on what kind of materials the builders could gather.

THE COLOSSEUM

Rome, Italy

In the center of Rome stands one of the largest and most impressive ancient Roman buildings. The construction of the Colosseum started between 72 and 75 CE, and it opened in 80 CE. Much of the Colosseum is made of concrete—at the time a brand-new material that the Romans had only just started using.

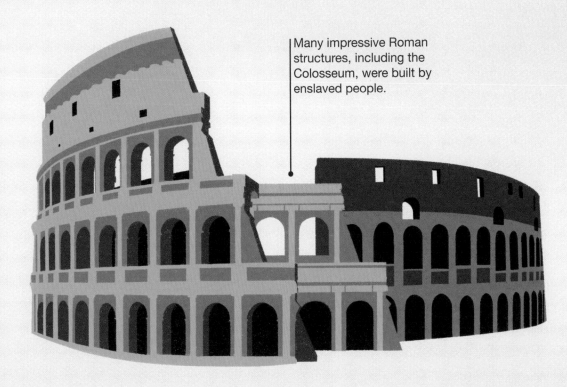

Many impressive Roman structures, including the Colosseum, were built by enslaved people.

ANGKOR WAT

Cambodia

Angkor Wat translates to "City of Temples." It was built in the 12th century and remains the largest religious monument in the world. The builders used up to 10 million blocks of sandstone, which came from a quarry about 22 miles/35 kilometers away. These were floated down the river on sturdy rafts. The complex and the surrounding city was larger than modern-day Paris. Virtually every wall, column, and even roof is covered in detailed carvings.

Bricks were bound together using an almost invisible glue made from plant matter instead of mortar.

Treadwheel cranes were used in the Middle Ages. A person or animal would be placed in the central wheel—a little like a hamster wheel—to power them.

CRANES

Cranes were first used by the ancient Greeks and Romans and mostly moved things from side to side. It was only in 13th-century Europe that cranes were first used to lift objects up and down. Early cranes were made of wood, but during the Industrial Revolution, in the 18th and 19th centuries, people began building them out of iron and steel to make them stronger.

Cranes are so called because they resemble the long neck of the crane bird.

THE GREAT SPHINX
Giza, Egypt

In the shadow of the pyramids at Giza is a giant statue of the Sphinx, a mythical creature with the body of a lion and the head of a human. The Great Sphinx is a monolith, meaning it was carved from a single huge piece of rock. In Egyptian mythology, sphinxes protected tombs and temples, and this particular one was completed at about the same time as the pyramid tombs it was built to protect. It is believed that the same skilled workers who built the pyramids between 2550 and 2490 BCE also carved out the Sphinx.

For most of its history, the Sphinx has been buried up to its neck in the desert sand. Archaeologists began digging out the Sphinx in 1925.

The Sphinx looks east, to face the rising sun.

The Sphinx is 240 feet/73 meters long and 66 feet/20 meters high.

MONOLITH
The limestone block that became the Sphinx was too soft to be used in the construction of the nearby pyramids.

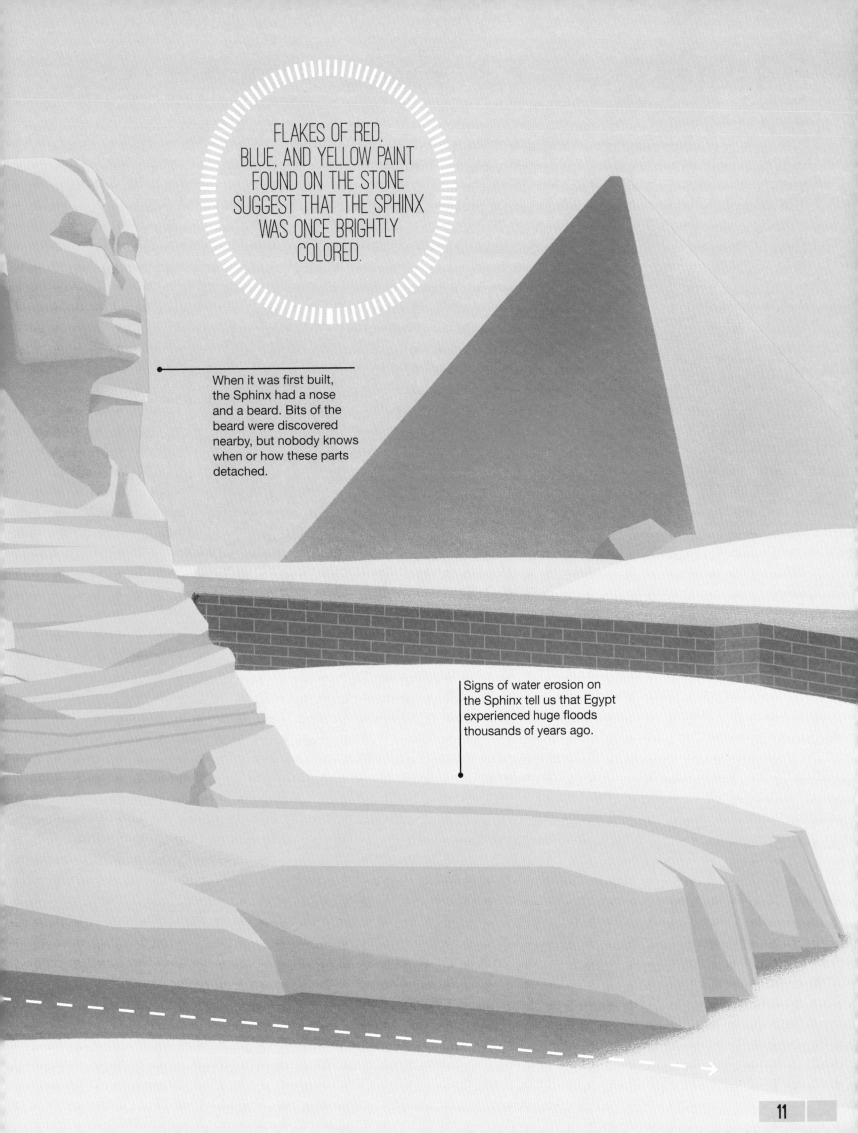

FLAKES OF RED, BLUE, AND YELLOW PAINT FOUND ON THE STONE SUGGEST THAT THE SPHINX WAS ONCE BRIGHTLY COLORED.

When it was first built, the Sphinx had a nose and a beard. Bits of the beard were discovered nearby, but nobody knows when or how these parts detached.

Signs of water erosion on the Sphinx tell us that Egypt experienced huge floods thousands of years ago.

BRIDGES

Traveling from one place to another often means having to cross obstacles like rivers, deep valleys, or roads. To get across these, bridges need to be built. There are several ancient bridges still standing today. The Arkadiko Bridge in Greece is more than 3,000 years old, and the Zhaozhou Bridge in China was built about 1,500 years ago. Today, bridges can stretch for many miles, tower hundreds of feet tall, and are often iconic features of the surrounding landscape.

DANYANG-KUNSHAN GRAND BRIDGE

Shanghai to Nanjing, China

At just under 103 miles/165 kilometers long, this arch bridge is the longest bridge in the world. It's part of a railway link between Beijing and Nanjing, allowing people to travel across a huge area full of marshes, rivers, lakes, and canals. It took 10,000 people four years to build and opened in 2011.

The bridge is supported by a staggering 9,500 concrete pilings.

← **103 miles/165 kilometers from Shanghai to Nanjing**

TOWER BRIDGE

London, England

Tower Bridge in London is one of the best-known sights in the city. It was built between 1886 and 1894. It is a suspension bridge and also a bascule bridge, meaning the section between the two towers can open to allow large ships to pass underneath.

Cars aren't allowed to drive more than 20 miles/32 kilometers per hour across the bridge to avoid damaging the structure.

There was a competition to design Tower Bridge, with over 50 entries.

PROBLEMS WITH BUILDING BRIDGES

Bridges need to be strong enough to survive severe storms and support the traffic that crosses them. A bridge built for people to cross on foot will not be able to hold large trucks. The design of a bridge and the materials used can vary depending on how strong it needs to be.

As bridges are exposed to bad weather and heavy traffic, they have to be constantly checked to make sure they are still safe. Modern engineers use high-tech equipment such as sensors to examine the strength of bridges and to look for weak points that may need to be repaired.

DIFFERENT KINDS OF BRIDGES

The simplest type of bridge is a beam bridge. This is just a single beam lying across an obstacle like a river. It may have pillars underneath to support it and is good for crossing short distances. A truss bridge, such as the Quebec Bridge in Canada, uses metal or wooden poles that cross each other to support the weight of the bridge. Arch bridges use large arches to spread out the weight of the structure, while suspension bridges have tall towers that hold up the main body with huge steel cables. Cantilever bridges, first built in the 19th century, use cantilevers, or structures that project into space and are anchored at only one end.

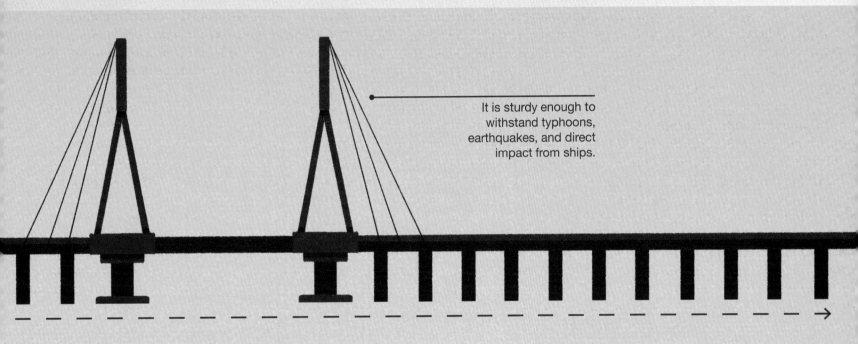

It is sturdy enough to withstand typhoons, earthquakes, and direct impact from ships.

THE SYDNEY HARBOUR BRIDGE

Sydney, Australia

Nicknamed "The Coathanger" by locals, this iconic steel arch bridge took eight years and 58,400 tons/53,000 metric tons of steel to build. Each of the six million rivets holding the bridge together was handmade. The original plan was to build a cantilever bridge, but plans were delayed by the First World War, and by the time work was ready to start, improvements to steel making made arch bridges easier and faster to build.

Spanning 3,770 feet/1,149 meters, Sydney Harbour Bridge is one of the longest steel arch bridges in the world. The arch itself is 1,650 feet/503 meters.

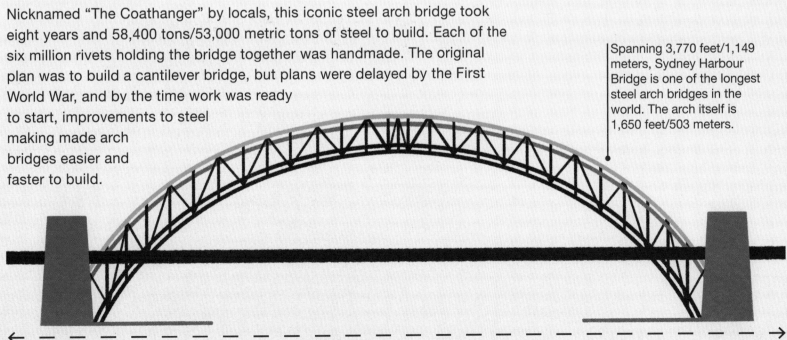

1,650 feet/503 meters

CABLES

The bridge has two main cables that are each over 1 mile/2 kilometers long and about 3 feet/1 meter wide. Each cable is made up of over 27,000 wires wrapped together. If you laid all the wires end to end, they would encircle the world three times.

3 feet/0.93 meters

There were special safety nets under the bridge during construction. They saved the lives of many workers.

GOLDEN GATE BRIDGE
San Francisco, USA

The Golden Gate strait connects the Pacific Ocean and San Francisco Bay. The Golden Gate Bridge was built so that people could cross the strait on their way to and from the city of San Francisco. Construction started on both sides of the strait at the start of 1933. Strong winds, stormy waters, and thick fog made the job of building the bridge difficult and dangerous, but it finally opened in 1937. At over 8,900 feet/2,700 meters long and nearly 750 feet/230 meters high, it was both the highest and longest suspension bridge in the world at the time. It is now seen as one of most the most famous bridges in the world.

The bridge is painted in international orange. This color helps to make the bridge visible when it is foggy.

FILMMAKERS LOVE TO DEMOLISH THE BRIDGE. IT'S BEEN DESTROYED IN STAR TREK, X-MEN, AND SUPERMAN MOVIES.

The Golden Gate Bridge is designed to withstand huge earthquakes, like the devastating 1906 San Francisco Earthquake. In 1989, the nearby Bay Bridge collapsed in an earthquake, while the Golden Gate Bridge suffered only minor damage.

The bridge was built 220 feet/67 meters above the water to allow large boats to pass underneath.

SKYSCRAPERS

A skyscraper is not just a tall building. Some ancient civilizations had structures five to six stories tall—impressive in an age when most buildings were only one to two stories high. Skyscrapers only started to be built around 100 years ago. They have steel frames, which hold up the structure. The outer surfaces are then covered in "curtain walls" and can be made of light materials such as glass because they do not take any structural weight.

WHY BUILD SKYSCRAPERS?

Skyscrapers are normally found in the center of cities, where land for new buildings is not readily available and is very expensive. Skyscrapers create more space by building upward instead of outward.

PROBLEMS BUILDING SKYSCRAPERS

The main problem with skyscrapers is that they are very heavy and risk falling over or sinking into the ground. To solve this, the steel frame of the building rests on an underground steel-and-concrete base, which carries the weight. New, lighter materials and innovative design have allowed for the construction of taller skyscrapers.

All skyscrapers have to be strong enough to hold up against high winds and are built to sway slightly when the wind is strong. They are also designed to withstand disasters such as earthquakes and fires.

GOING UP AND DOWN

The safety elevator (which won't fall even if the cable holding it breaks) was invented in 1853, and the first electric elevator was built in 1880. Very high skyscrapers have express elevators that only stop at a few floors—just like an express train! People can then move to another elevator that stops at every floor.

BURJ KHALIFA
Dubai, United Arab Emirates

Not only is this 2,717-foot/828-meter tower the tallest building in the world, but it has also broken many other records. It has the highest outdoor observation deck (1,821 feet/555 meters above the ground), the highest occupied floor (the 160th) and the longest elevator ride in the world. An enormous amount of concrete and aluminum was used to build the tower.

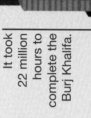

It took 22 million hours to complete the Burj Khalifa.

EMPIRE STATE BUILDING
New York City, USA

The Empire State Building was completed in 1931, at a time when many skyscrapers were being constructed and the competition to put up the world's tallest building was fierce. At just over 1,450 feet/440 meters tall, this art deco icon beat New York's Chrysler Building and 40 Wall Street for the title, which it held for nearly 40 years. It was also the first skyscraper to have more than 100 floors.

PETRONAS TWIN TOWERS
Kuala Lumpur, Malaysia

At 1,483 feet/452 meters high, these twin skyscrapers were the tallest buildings in the world between 1998 and 2004, before they were overtaken by Taipei 101 in Taiwan. They are still the world's tallest twin towers. The sky bridge, which links them and is used as an observation platform, stands a dizzying 558 feet/170 meters off the ground. They also have the deepest foundations in the world.

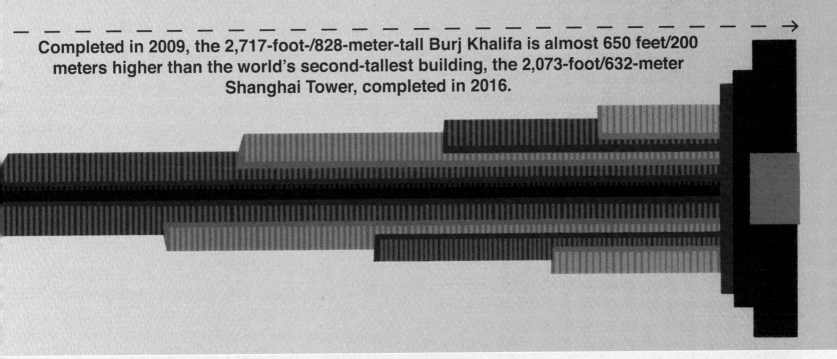

Completed in 2009, the 2,717-foot-/828-meter-tall Burj Khalifa is almost 650 feet/200 meters higher than the world's second-tallest building, the 2,073-foot/632-meter Shanghai Tower, completed in 2016.

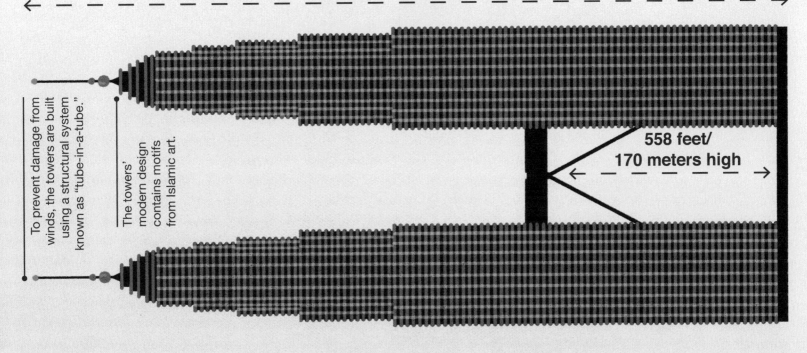

1,483 feet/452 meters high

To prevent damage from winds, the towers are built using a structural system known as "tube-in-a-tube."

The towers' modern design contains motifs from Islamic art.

558 feet/
170 meters high

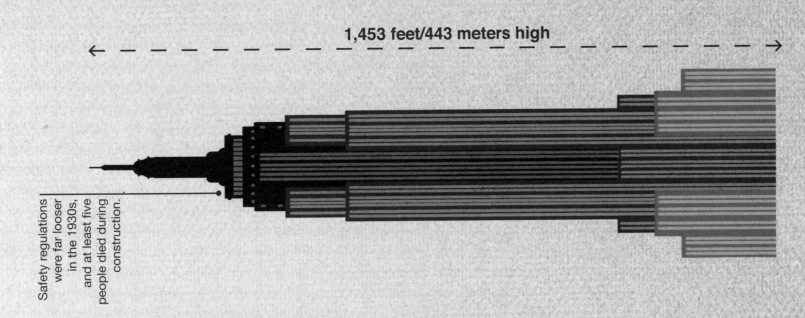

1,453 feet/443 meters high

Safety regulations were far looser in the 1930s, and at least five people died during construction.

THE SHARD

London, England

When the UK government decided to replace Southwark Towers, a run-down 1970s office building by the River Thames, with a new skyscraper, they stated that they wanted to choose a new building of "exceptional design." The Shard, a 1,016-foot/310-meter giant of glass and steel, certainly meets that requirement. Covered with treated glass, it is angled to reflect the sunlight and the blue sky, providing a shining addition to the London skyline. The skyscraper's eye-catching, modern design was first sketched by architect Renzo Piano in the year 2000 on the back of a menu in a restaurant in Berlin, Germany. It was met with criticism from English Heritage, an organization that manages historic properties, which described it as a "shard of glass through the heart of historic London." Renzo Piano liked this cutting description so much that he chose it as the skyscraper's name.

The penthouse apartment covers two floors and is approximately the same size as a seven-bedroom mansion.

The building's exterior contains 11,000 panes of glass, which, if laid out, would cover eight soccer fields.

1,017 feet/310 meters tall

DURING CONSTRUCTION, BUILDERS RESCUED A FOX THAT HAD MANAGED TO REACH THE 72ND FLOOR.

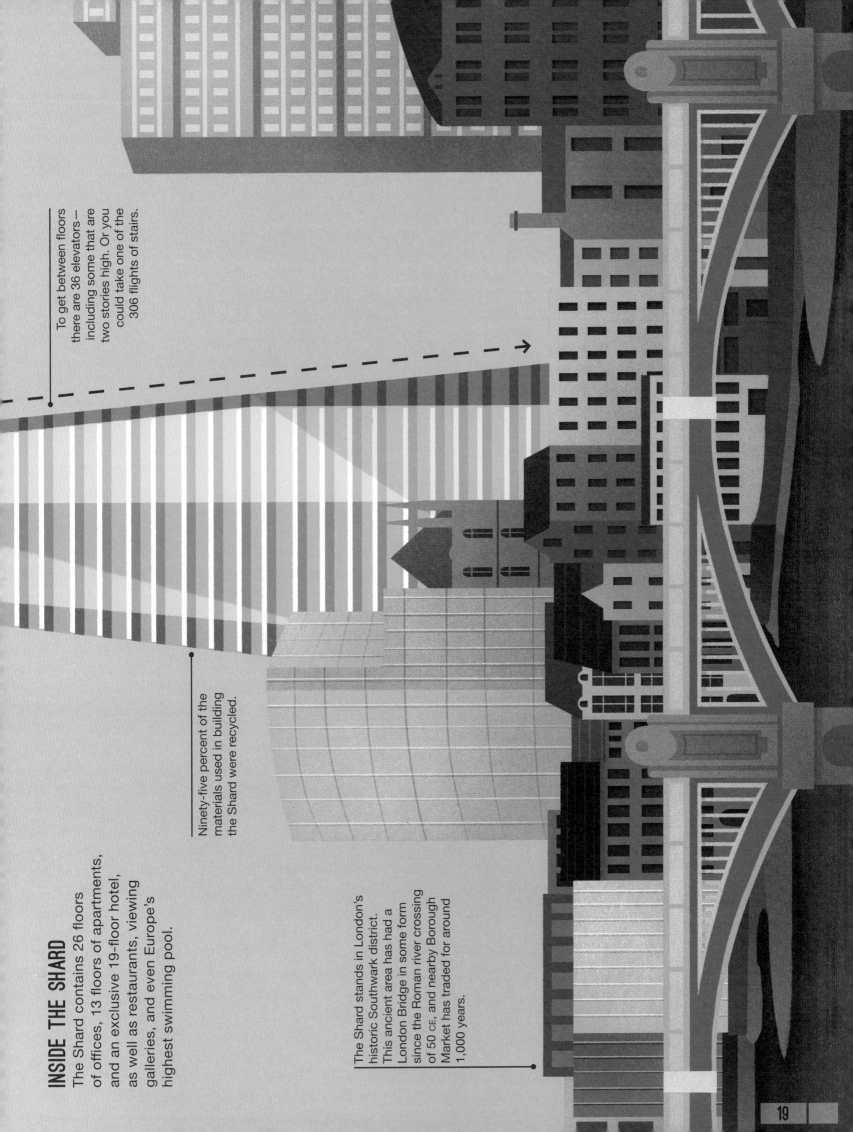

INSIDE THE SHARD

The Shard contains 26 floors of offices, 13 floors of apartments, and an exclusive 19-floor hotel, as well as restaurants, viewing galleries, and even Europe's highest swimming pool.

To get between floors there are 36 elevators—including some that are two stories high. Or you could take one of the 306 flights of stairs.

Ninety-five percent of the materials used in building the Shard were recycled.

The Shard stands in London's historic Southwark district. This ancient area has had a London Bridge in some form since the Roman river crossing of 50 CE, and nearby Borough Market has traded for around 1,000 years.

ENGINEERING IN SPACE

The exploration of space started in 1957 when the Soviet Union launched the first satellite, Sputnik 1. In 1961, Russian cosmonaut Yuri Gagarin became the first person in space, and eight years later, Neil Armstrong, an American astronaut, became the first person to walk on the moon. There are many unique problems that space engineers must overcome, particularly the lack of gravity and oxygen in the expanse of space.

SATURN V

Earth to the Moon

On July 20, 1969, astronauts Neil Armstrong and Edwin "Buzz" Aldrin became the first people to walk on the moon. Their rocket, Saturn V, was mostly made up of fuel tanks, which separated from the main body and fell away as the fuel was used up. Only the 10-foot-/3-meter-high command module returned to Earth.

Saturn V used an enormous 23 tons/20.9 metric tons of fuel per second.

Over 330 feet/100 meters tall

The rocket was made up of three parts. Only the top part with astronauts inside would make it into space.

Weighing over 3,300 tons/3,000 metric tons when fully fueled up, Saturn V needed a specially designed transporter to get it to the launch site.

ALL THE CALCULATIONS NEEDED TO SEND THE APOLLO 11 MISSION TO THE MOON WERE DONE BY HAND, WITHOUT THE HELP OF COMPUTERS.

GRAVITY AND LIFT-OFF

A rocket taking off has to be fast enough to escape Earth's gravity. This is called escape velocity. On Earth, a rocket has to travel over 7 miles/11 kilometers per second to get into space.

Once in space, there is little or no gravity at all. Many machines and tools won't work in space because of this. Everyday tasks like eating or going to the bathroom need to be carefully planned.

DUST PARTICLES

Tiny particles of dust move through the vacuum of space. This can badly damage sensitive instruments if they come into contact with spacecraft. Spacecraft also have to avoid all of the nearly 1,500 satellites that are currently orbiting Earth.

WATER AND AIR

Water and air are essential for life, but both are very hard to come by in space. On space stations, oxygen is extracted from water or recycled from the air astronauts breathe out. Until recently, water was recycled from the breath, sweat, and even urine of astronauts. Today the Sabatier system creates water from the waste gases hydrogen and carbon dioxide instead.

New Horizons used Jupiter's gravity to speed up by an extra 9,000 miles/14,000 kilometers per hour.

NEW HORIZONS
Earth to Pluto

In January 2006, the New Horizons space probe was launched. It arrived at the dwarf planet Pluto ten years and more than 3 billion miles/ 5 billion kilometers later. This might seem like a long time, but New Horizons is the fastest spacecraft ever launched.

It took the Apollo mission three days to reach the moon. Traveling at 10 miles/ 16 kilometers per second, New Horizons made the same trip in nine hours.

SPACE SHUTTLE
Reusable Rocket

Rockets like Saturn V were very wasteful and expensive, as they could only be used once. In 1981, the first space shuttle was launched. This spacecraft could be used several times. It still needed huge rockets to get it into space, but once it returned to Earth, it could be steered like a plane and land on a runway. The last space shuttle flew in 2011.

Space shuttles also served as portable laboratories so astronauts could do experiments in microgravity.

In orbit, space shuttles traveled at 17,400 miles/ 28,000 kilometers per hour. At this speed, astronauts could see a sunrise and sunset every 45 minutes!

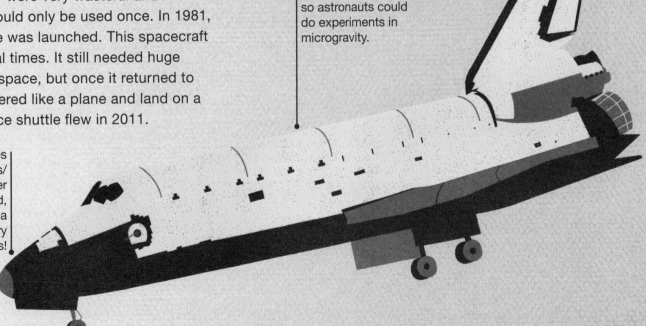

INTERNATIONAL SPACE STATION

250 miles/400 kilometers above Earth

Hundreds of miles above the Earth, traveling at over 17,400 miles/28,000 kilometers per hour, is the International Space Station. This is a modular space station, which means it is made up of many different sections that were built on Earth and then assembled in space. The first section, Zarya, was built by the Russians in 1998. The American-built section, Unity, was added later in the same year. Many more sections have been added since then. People have been living and working on the ISS since 2000.

The ISS is powered by sunlight. Its solar arrays convert the light to electricity. The solar arrays are panels made up of thousands of silicone solar cells. The space station has 27,000 square feet/2,500 square meters of solar arrays and each is 240 feet/73 meters long—similar in length to a Boeing 777 aircraft.

The ISS travels at 5 miles/ 8 kilometers per second. It circles the Earth every 90 minutes.

The space station can support a crew of six astronauts plus visitors. Inside are living quarters and laboratories.

Robotic arms attached to the outside of the ISS help build and repair parts of the space station. They've even been used to move astronauts around.

INTERNATIONAL COOPERATION

The ISS has been built and is still maintained by a group of space agencies from Russia, the USA, Canada, Japan, and the European Union. The ISS is an incredible feat of both engineering and international cooperation, as it is the first time multiple countries have worked together in the pursuit of knowledge of our cosmos.

The ISS is the third brightest object in our night sky, after the moon and Venus. You can often see it, and there is a website that tracks its location.

The modules of the ISS were sent to space on rockets. Other parts were transported in shuttles and put together in orbit during space walks.

AT 358 FEET / 109 METERS LONG, THE ISS IS THE LARGEST MANNED SATELLITE EVER PUT INTO SPACE.

TUNNELS

Many ancient civilizations, including the Egyptians, Persians, and Mesopotamians, built gently sloping tunnels, called qanats, to carry water for crops or provide drinking water for towns. The first qanats were built around 3,000 years ago. One of the first road tunnels was built in Italy during the Roman Empire and was nearly three-fifths of a mile or a kilometer long. Tunnels were once built with nothing but simple hand tools. Today explosives and huge boring machines are often used.

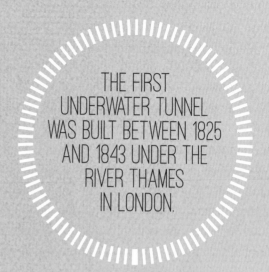

THE FIRST UNDERWATER TUNNEL WAS BUILT BETWEEN 1825 AND 1843 UNDER THE RIVER THAMES IN LONDON.

GOTTHARD BASE TUNNEL

The Alps, Switzerland

The world's longest railway tunnel is the Gotthard Base Tunnel in Switzerland. It runs for just over 35 miles/57 kilometers under the Alpine mountain range and was opened in 2016. There are already plans to build another tunnel alongside it.

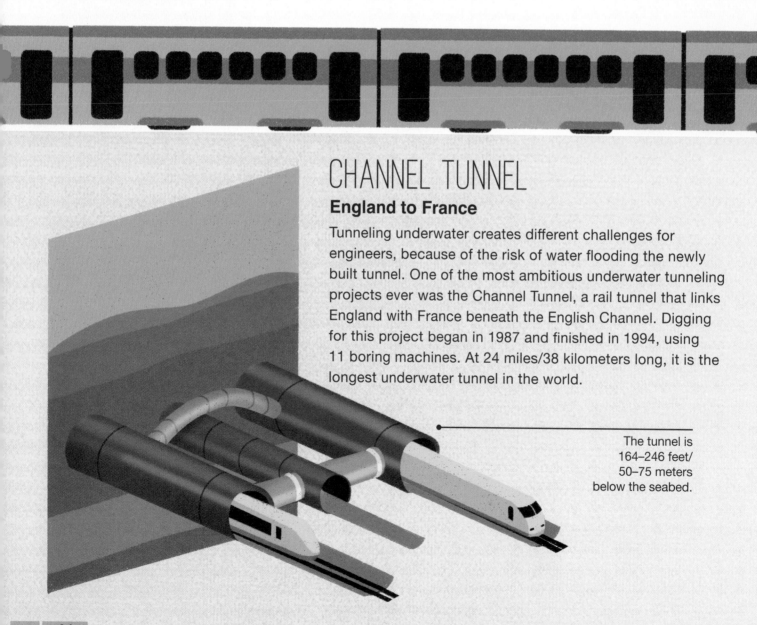

CHANNEL TUNNEL

England to France

Tunneling underwater creates different challenges for engineers, because of the risk of water flooding the newly built tunnel. One of the most ambitious underwater tunneling projects ever was the Channel Tunnel, a rail tunnel that links England with France beneath the English Channel. Digging for this project began in 1987 and finished in 1994, using 11 boring machines. At 24 miles/38 kilometers long, it is the longest underwater tunnel in the world.

The tunnel is 164–246 feet/ 50–75 meters below the seabed.

TUNNEL-DIGGING TECHNIQUES

Cut-and-cover is the simplest way to dig a tunnel. A long trench is dug out, and then a roof is built over the trench, leaving a tunnel inside. Most of the early underground systems were built using this cut-and-cover technique, and it has recently been used as part of London's Crossrail project—the largest infrastructure project in Europe. While it is quite straightforward, cut-and-cover can only be used for tunnels that are not too deep, and it cannot be used if the tunnel has to go through rock.

Boring machines (sometimes known as "moles") are circular cutting machines that can tunnel through soil and rock. The first boring machine was used in 1846 for the building of a railway tunnel between France and Italy. They are also used to build tunnels in modern cities, as the cut-and-cover method would mean that busy roads would have to be closed.

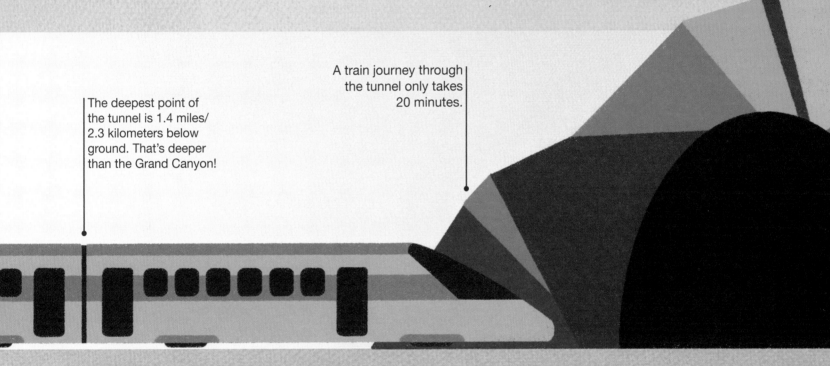

The deepest point of the tunnel is 1.4 miles/ 2.3 kilometers below ground. That's deeper than the Grand Canyon!

A train journey through the tunnel only takes 20 minutes.

BERTHA

Seattle, USA

The biggest boring machine in the world, known as "Bertha," was over 57 feet/ 17.5 meters across. It was built to drill a road tunnel underneath Seattle, and was designed to drill through soft rock, like chalk and limestone, as opposed to hard rock, such as granite. This doesn't mean that Bertha had an easy time, though, as engineers had to find a way to stop dust and sand from getting into the machine and damaging it.

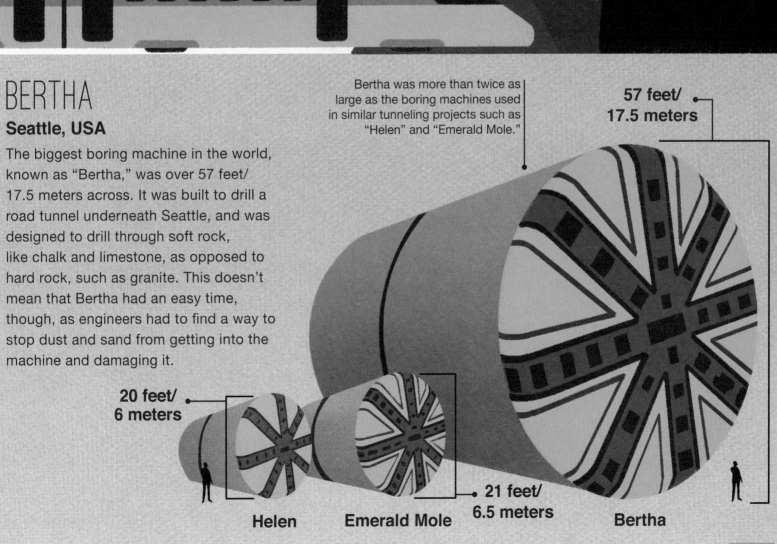

Bertha was more than twice as large as the boring machines used in similar tunneling projects such as "Helen" and "Emerald Mole."

57 feet/ 17.5 meters

20 feet/ 6 meters

21 feet/ 6.5 meters

Helen   **Emerald Mole**   **Bertha**

LONDON UNDERGROUND
London, England

The world's oldest underground railway system is the London Underground, known as "the Tube." The first part of the London Underground, the Metropolitan Line, was opened in 1863 and carried 40,000 passengers on opening day. At the time, the Underground used steam trains, which filled the air with dirty smoke. This meant that more than half of the tracks were actually built above ground, and the remaining tunnels had to be extremely well ventilated. In 1890, the steam trains were replaced by much cleaner electric trains. The early lines were built using the cut-and-cover method, but later lines used boring machines to avoid having to shut down streets with invasive building work.

MOSQUITOES HAVE BEEN LIVING IN THE TUNNELS FOR SO LONG THAT THEY HAVE EVOLVED INTO A SUBSPECIES OF MOSQUITO THAT IS NOT FOUND ANYWHERE ELSE.

Many of the underground lines follow the streets above them. This was because the private companies building the tunnels would have had to pay the owners of buildings to travel under them.

In the Second World War, London's Tube stations were used as air-raid shelters. Holborn and Aldwych stations were used to store and protect artifacts from the British Museum. Many lives were saved by these tunnels during the Blitz.

Hampstead station is the deepest station in London, located 192 feet/58.5 meters below the city. There are 320 stairs between the street and the platform.

The longest distance between two stations is 4 miles/6 kilometers, and the shortest is 853 feet/260 meters.

Each Tube train travels around 114,500 miles/184,300 kilometers every year—that's nearly five trips around the world.

THE TUBE NETWORK

Today, the London Underground has 270 stations and 250 miles/402 kilometers of railway track, sprawling across the whole city. The number of daily passengers has grown to 5,000,000.

CANALS

Canals are human-made channels of water, which serve many different purposes. Smaller canals offer transport through cities like Venice, Amsterdam, and Bangkok, while other, larger canals make it easier to carry goods from one place to another. The Lehigh Canal in the USA, for example, was built to transport coal from Pennsylvania. Canals may also provide shortcuts between two large bodies of water, such as the Suez Canal, which connects the Mediterranean to the Indian Ocean via the Red Sea, and the Panama Canal which connects the Atlantic and the Pacific oceans (pages 30–31). They can also provide water for farming and accessible drinking water to remote areas.

TRAVELING UP AND DOWN

Canals often go through land that is not flat. As water can only travel downhill, engineers have had to find a way to ensure boats can travel in any direction. Many canals use locks to solve this problem. These are two large gates across the canal with a large gap between them. The gates are opened, allowing water to flow in or out, and then closed to keep the water at one level so the boat can sail through smoothly.

OVERCOMING OBSTACLES

Sometimes, canals come across an obstruction, such as a deep valley or river. To cross these, engineers developed aqueducts— bridges with water running along the top—so boats can continue traveling along the canal safely and easily.

BANGKOK CANAL, THAILAND

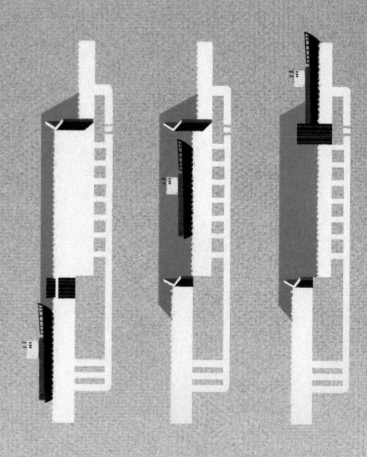

The Kieldrecht Lock took three times more steel to build than the Eiffel Tower in Paris.

RECORD BREAKERS

Kieldrecht Lock, Belgium

Until recently, the largest lock in the world was the Berendrecht Lock in the port of Antwerp in Belgium. In 2016, this record was taken by another lock in the same area, the Kieldrecht Lock. Both of these locks allow large, ocean-going ships to access the docks.

THE WORLD'S LONGEST CANAL
Grand Canal, China

At 1,104 miles/1,776 kilometers long, the longest canal in the world is the Grand Canal in China. It is also the oldest canal in the world, with parts dating as far back as 500 BCE.

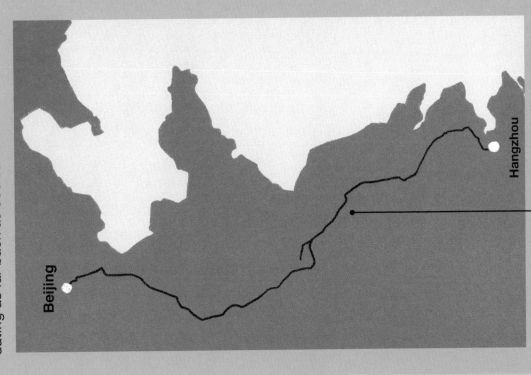

Beijing

Hangzhou

The canal crosses through cities and mountains to connect the Yellow and Yangtze Rivers.

LOTS OF LOCKS
Kennet and Avon Canal, England

When the Kennet and Avon Canal in England was built around 200 years ago, it had to be built up a steep hill, nearly 2.5 miles/4 kilometers long. Engineers decided to build a series of 29 locks along this stretch of the canal. Today, it usually takes about five hours for a boat to traverse all of these locks.

THE CITY WITH THE MOST MILES OF CANALS IS BIRMINGHAM, ENGLAND, WITH 35 MILES/ 56 KILOMETERS OF CANAL THROUGHOUT THE CITY.

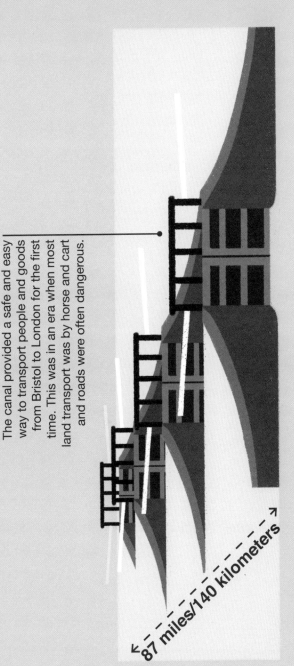

The canal provided a safe and easy way to transport people and goods from Bristol to London for the first time. This was in an era when most land transport was by horse and cart and roads were often dangerous.

87 miles/140 kilometers

FACING CHALLENGES

One of the main problems faced by engineers when building canals is that they have to be dug through many different types of soil. Canal builders can find themselves facing rocky areas that very quickly become sandy, or flat areas that turn steep.

Explosives are often used to blast through hard, rocky ground. Soft and sandy ground causes further challenges, as it cannot hold water. To solve this, canals have to be lined with waterproof clay or concrete known as puddle clay.

Some canals may also have to be built through mountainous areas. Usually, canals are simply built around hills and mountains, even if this makes journeys longer. Occasionally, though, tunnels are built through the mountain. These are usually quite short because, until recently, the boats using them had no engines, so the crew had to push them through.

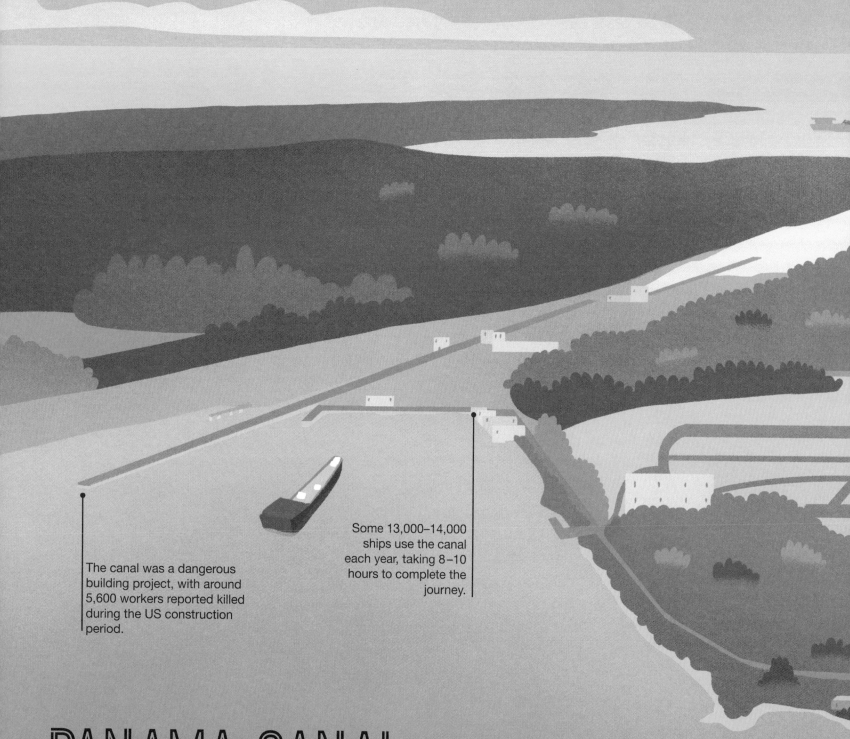

The canal was a dangerous building project, with around 5,600 workers reported killed during the US construction period.

Some 13,000–14,000 ships use the canal each year, taking 8–10 hours to complete the journey.

PANAMA CANAL

East to west coast, Panama

For centuries, the only route between the Atlantic and Pacific Oceans was to sail around the far south coast of South America. It was a long and often dangerous journey. The French government decided that the best solution was to build a canal across a thin strip of land in Central America. This canal would reduce the traveling time between the Atlantic and Pacific to less than a day. Work on the Panama Canal was started by France in 1881, but was abandoned because of engineering problems. The USA took over construction in 1904, and it was completed 10 years later. Even today, it is seen as one of the most difficult engineering projects ever undertaken.

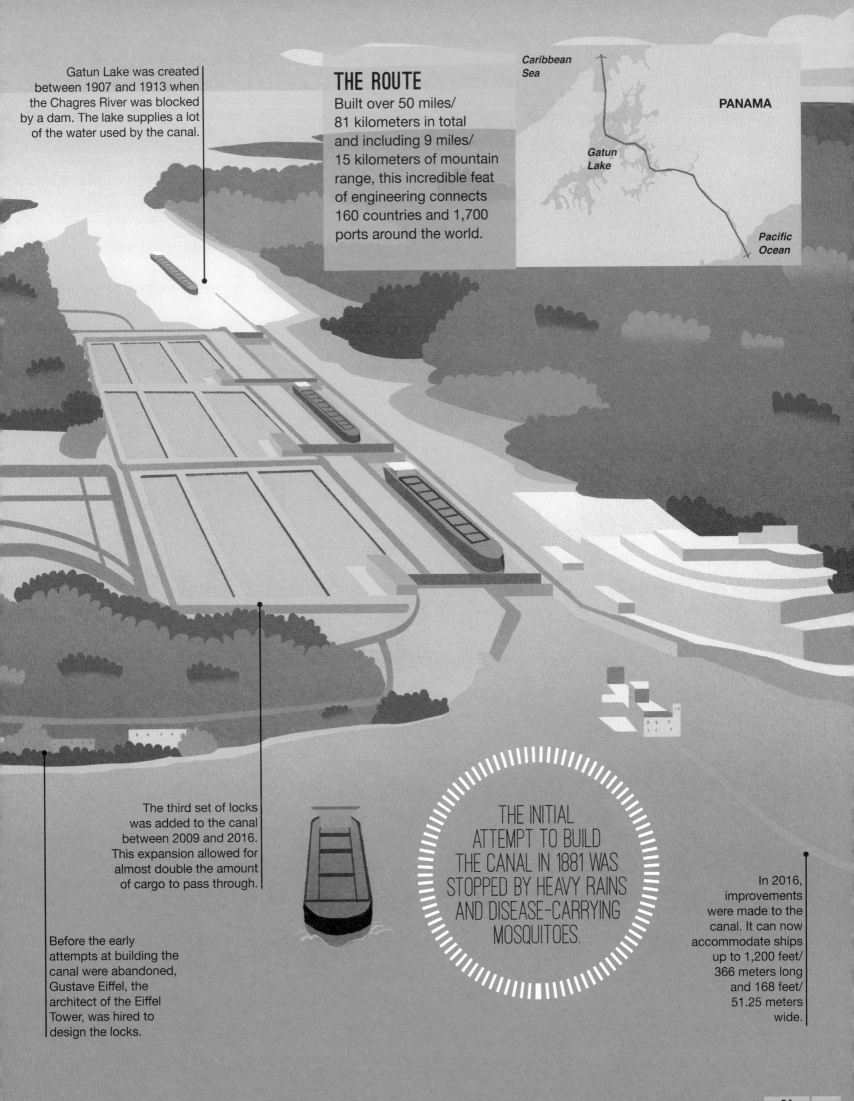

Gatun Lake was created between 1907 and 1913 when the Chagres River was blocked by a dam. The lake supplies a lot of the water used by the canal.

THE ROUTE

Built over 50 miles/ 81 kilometers in total and including 9 miles/ 15 kilometers of mountain range, this incredible feat of engineering connects 160 countries and 1,700 ports around the world.

Caribbean Sea

PANAMA

Gatun Lake

Pacific Ocean

The third set of locks was added to the canal between 2009 and 2016. This expansion allowed for almost double the amount of cargo to pass through.

Before the early attempts at building the canal were abandoned, Gustave Eiffel, the architect of the Eiffel Tower, was hired to design the locks.

THE INITIAL ATTEMPT TO BUILD THE CANAL IN 1881 WAS STOPPED BY HEAVY RAINS AND DISEASE-CARRYING MOSQUITOES.

In 2016, improvements were made to the canal. It can now accommodate ships up to 1,200 feet/ 366 meters long and 168 feet/ 51.25 meters wide.

CREATING ENERGY

The demand for energy is constantly growing. This is because the world's population is getting bigger, and because people are using more devices that require power, such as mobile phones, computers, cars, and central heating. Today, over half of the world's energy comes from coal and oil, which produce carbon dioxide, a gas that gets trapped in Earth's atmosphere, contributing to climate change. To continue to meet demand while minimizing carbon dioxide production, engineers must find new ways to create, conserve, and store clean, renewable energy.

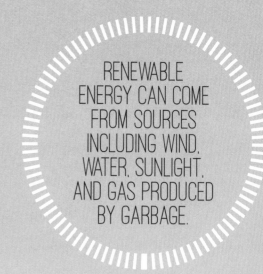

RENEWABLE ENERGY CAN COME FROM SOURCES INCLUDING WIND, WATER, SUNLIGHT, AND GAS PRODUCED BY GARBAGE.

GANSU WIND FARM

Gansu Province, China

The world's largest wind farm is the Gansu Wind Farm in China. Construction began in 2009. It has over 7,000 wind turbines, and new turbines are still being added. Engineers plan for it to eventually power millions of homes.

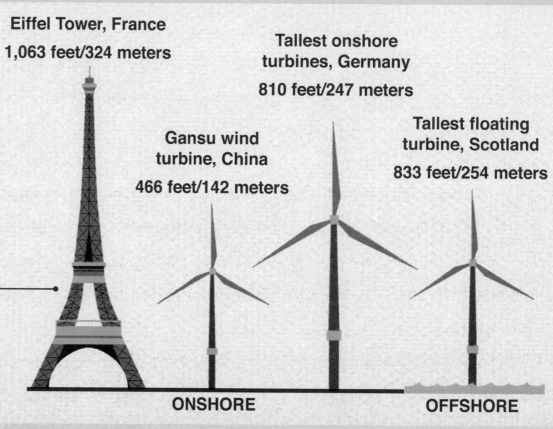

Eiffel Tower, France
1,063 feet/324 meters

Tallest onshore turbines, Germany
810 feet/247 meters

Gansu wind turbine, China
466 feet/142 meters

Tallest floating turbine, Scotland
833 feet/254 meters

Wind turbines can be enormous, with the tallest reaching almost the same height as the Eiffel Tower.

ONSHORE

OFFSHORE

SIHWA LAKE

Gyeonggi-do Province, South Korea

Tidal barrages convert energy produced by the oceans' tides into electricity. South Korea boasts the world's largest tidal barrage, Sihwa Lake Tidal Power Station. Here, 10 massive turbines are turned by the changing tides, creating enough electricity for half a million homes.

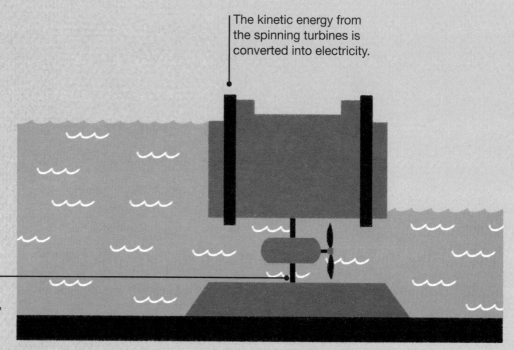

The kinetic energy from the spinning turbines is converted into electricity.

Water is pushed through huge turbines, causing them to spin.

RENEWABLE ENERGY

Renewable energy comes from several different sources. Hydroelectricity produces energy using water. Engineers build enormous dams across rivers, and the force of the water moving through the dam spins the blades of giant turbines inside it. This creates kinetic energy, which can then be converted into electricity. Tidal barrages work in a similar way, using the force of ocean tides to spin the barrages' turbines.

Solar power uses light and heat from the sun. One widespread method of doing this is to use large panels made up of small photovoltaic cells. These convert the sun's energy into electricity.

Many new homes are built with their own solar panels, and engineers also build solar parks with thousands of panels.

Wind power works by capturing kinetic energy from the wind and turning it into electricity. The most common way of doing this is by using wind turbines. Large groups of wind turbines are known as wind farms. Some wind farms, known as offshore farms, are several miles out to sea, where winds can reach very high speeds. The largest offshore wind farm is the Walney Wind Farm, 12 miles/ 19 kilometers off the coast of Cumbria, England.

Hydrogen may also be a key renewable fuel for the future. It can be combined with oxygen to generate heat, electricity, and water.

THREE GORGES DAM

Yangtze River, China

The Three Gorges Dam is the largest hydroelectric dam in the world. Work started in 1994 and finished in 2006. Over a million people were displaced to accommodate its construction. The Three Gorges Dam is over 1 mile/ 2 kilometers long and nearly 650 feet/200 meters high.

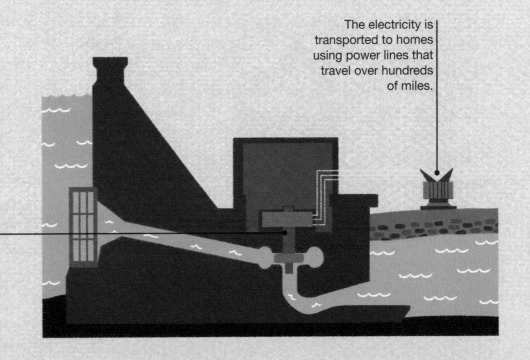

The electricity is transported to homes using power lines that travel over hundreds of miles.

Energy from the spinning turbines is converted into electricity.

KAMUTHI PROJECT

Kamuthi, India

The Kamuthi Solar Power Project is one of the largest solar farms in the world. It covers about 4 square miles/10 square kilometers and contains 2.5 million solar panels. The whole site was built in 2016, and took just eight months to build. The solar farm at Kamuthi creates enough electricity for 750,000 people.

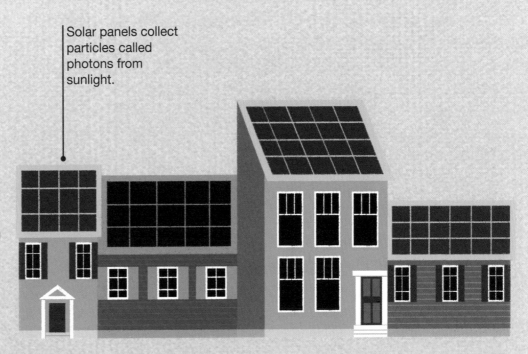

Solar panels collect particles called photons from sunlight.

HOOVER DAM
Colorado River, USA

In the 1930s, the world went through the Great Depression. This was a time of economic crisis, and millions of people around the world lost their jobs and their homes. In the USA, President Franklin D. Roosevelt helped create work for as many people as possible by ordering large engineering and building projects under an initiative known as the New Deal. One of these projects was the Hoover Dam on the Colorado River. Work started on the dam in 1931 and finished in 1936, with over 20,000 people working on it during this time. As well as providing electricity, it was also used to supply water to local farmers and factories.

The dam is over 725 feet/220 meters high and nearly 1,300 feet/400 meters long.

When the dam was completed, it created Lake Mead. This is the largest reservoir (artificial lake) in the USA.

When it was finished, it was the largest hydroelectric dam in the world and the largest concrete structure ever built. The largest dam today is the Three Gorges Dam in China (page 33).

BOULDER CITY

An entire town was built to house the headquarters and the workers who built the dam. Boulder City, perched on the side of the canyon, is still standing today, with a population of around 16,000 people.

Almost 9 million pounds/ 4 million kilograms of dynamite were used to blast the rocks on either side of the river before the dam could be built.

A GIANT REFRIGERATOR WAS DESIGNED TO COOL THE HUGE BLOCKS OF CONCRETE; OTHERWISE IT COULD HAVE TAKEN YEARS LONGER TO COMPLETE.

3,250,000 cubic yards/ 2,484,803 cubic meters of concrete were used to build the dam—enough to build 3,000 miles/4,800 kilometers of road.

RAILWAYS

The earliest railways were built around the 16th century and were powered by horses, which pulled wagons along wooden tracks. Toward the end of the 18th century, metal tracks were built to carry heavier weights. Around the same time, engineers began developing steam-powered engines as a new form of transport. Railways allowed many people to travel long distances in comfort for the first time.

ELECTRIC TRAM, LISBON, PORTUGAL

STEPHENSON'S ROCKET

The first successful steam train was built by British engineer Richard Trevithick in 1804. Twenty-five years later, father and son engineers George and Robert Stephenson built an improved steam train, called the Rocket. Stephenson's Rocket influenced the design for steam trains all over the world. In the 1820s, Britain and the USA began building railways to connect major cities. Railways began spreading across Europe by the 1830s and Asia by the 1870s.

Steam engines burned coal for energy, releasing thick black smoke into the atmosphere.

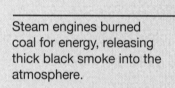

Rocket can be seen today in the National Railway Museum in York, England.

When a bullet train exits a tunnel at high speed, it makes a noise so loud it can knock a freight train over.

Engineers have built a 12-mile/20-kilometer track leading nowhere to test new bullet trains.

BUILDING RAILWAYS

Building railway lines is always a test of skill for engineers. Railways need to cover long distances and potentially cross varying landscapes such as rivers, mountain ranges, and marshland. Their popularity has led to major breakthroughs in tunnel building (pages 24–27) and bridge building (pages 12–15).

German engineer Ernst Werner von Siemens demonstrated the first electric train in Berlin in 1879. Trains and trams powered by electricity soon became a common sight in many cities, including New York, London, and Lisbon.

In the 1920s and 1930s, diesel-electric engines were first introduced in the USSR, Germany, and the USA, and they became widespread after the Second World War. Today, nearly all long-distance trains use diesel engines.

The highest railway in the world is in China. Opened in 2006, the nearly 1,200-mile/2,000-kilometer line connects the north of China with Tibet. This record-breaking railway contains the highest point on any railway line, the highest train station, and the highest railway tunnel. The trains were specially built to deal with altitudes. Because oxygen is thinner on these high-altitude routes, passengers are given their own oxygen supply.

FIRST TRANSCONTINENTAL RAILROAD

Nebraska to California, USA

Before the construction of this railway, large swathes of the USA were difficult to travel across. The journey had to be taken by wagon, crossing difficult and dangerous terrain, and could take weeks. This 1,776-mile/2,858-kilometer railroad, built between 1863 and 1869, allowed people to travel from the West Coast to Omaha, Nebraska, in only a week. From there, they could catch a train all the way to the East Coast.

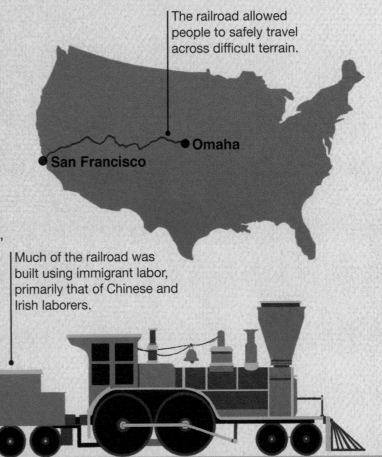

The railroad allowed people to safely travel across difficult terrain.

Omaha

San Francisco

Much of the railroad was built using immigrant labor, primarily that of Chinese and Irish laborers.

There has never been a fatal crash on Japan's bullet trains, making them one of the safest ways to travel.

BULLET TRAIN

Japan and China

Japan contains a network of high-speed electric trains called Shinkansen or bullet trains. These trains link many cities across Japan. Since they started in 1964, the Shinkansen have carried over 10 billion passengers. The trains can travel up to 199 miles/320 kilometers per hour. China now also has a high-speed railway, with trains traveling up to 217 miles/350 kilometers per hour.

To save money, many bridges were initially built with wood, and stations were built without foundations. This had to be changed later to prevent accidents.

In 1896, floods washed away almost 250 miles/400 kilometers of the track, which had to be repaired.

The longest tunnel on the railway is over 1 mile/ 2 kilometers long.

TRANS-SIBERIAN RAILWAY

Moscow to Vladivostok, Russia

The Trans-Siberian Railway has been the longest railway in the world for over a century. It connects Moscow in western Russia to Vladivostok in the east. It was originally built because travel across Russia, through the frozen and largely uninhabited area of Siberia, was slow and dangerous, especially in the winter. The main part of the line was built between 1891 and 1916. Workers began building at both ends and met in the middle. Today, the railway remains an important transport link for Russia. It is 5,772 miles/9,289 kilometers long—longer than the surviving section of the Great Wall of China—and takes eight days to travel from beginning to end.

THE RAILWAY IS A MAJOR PART OF RUSSIA'S ECONOMY, CARRYING AROUND 250,000 CONTAINERS OF GOODS EVERY YEAR.

It is estimated that 60,000 workers built the railway, which took 25 years to complete.

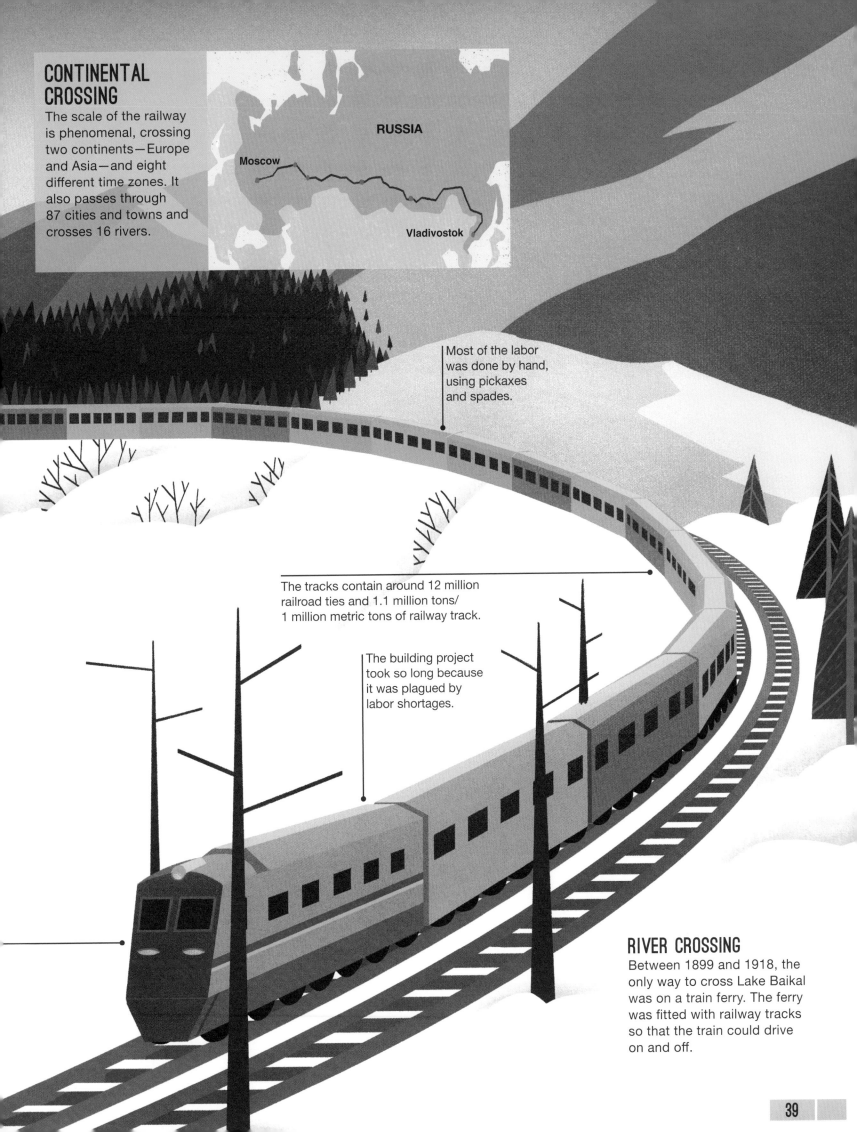

CONTINENTAL CROSSING

The scale of the railway is phenomenal, crossing two continents—Europe and Asia—and eight different time zones. It also passes through 87 cities and towns and crosses 16 rivers.

RUSSIA

Moscow

Vladivostok

Most of the labor was done by hand, using pickaxes and spades.

The tracks contain around 12 million railroad ties and 1.1 million tons/ 1 million metric tons of railway track.

The building project took so long because it was plagued by labor shortages.

RIVER CROSSING

Between 1899 and 1918, the only way to cross Lake Baikal was on a train ferry. The ferry was fitted with railway tracks so that the train could drive on and off.

BUILDING DEFENSES

Defensive engineering has existed for as long as people have gone to war. Some of the earliest human settlements in Europe, Asia, and the Middle East had defensive walls around them to protect the people who lived inside from attack. What is believed to be one of the oldest known defensive walls was built around the ancient Greek village of Sesklo almost 7,000 years ago. As settlements grew into cities and countries, defensive structures became bigger and more complex.

CASTLE SPIRAL STAIRWAYS WERE ALWAYS BUILT IN A CLOCKWISE DIRECTION SO SOLDIERS COULD EASILY DRAW THEIR SWORDS AS THEY RAN DOWNSTAIRS.

WALLS OF ÁVILA

Ávila, Spain

Some of the largest surviving defensive walls are around the city of Ávila. They were built not only to protect the residents of the city from enemy attack, but to limit who could come in and out to prevent the spread of the plague. Work started on the walls in 1090 and took about 300 years to complete. The rectangular walls are over 1 mile/2 kilometers long, 39 feet/ 12 meters high, and 10 feet/ 3 meters thick.

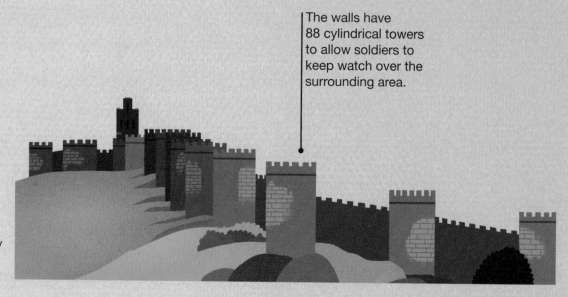

The walls have 88 cylindrical towers to allow soldiers to keep watch over the surrounding area.

FIRST WORLD WAR TRENCHES

Europe

In Europe, during the First World War (1914–1918), much of the conflict involved opposing soldiers facing each other in trenches. These trenches had to be deep enough for soldiers to safely walk around in—typically 10 feet/ 3 meters. Once tanks arrived on the battlefield in 1916, trenches became much harder to defend, and eventually armies had to adopt different strategies.

Soldiers tunneled between trenches to avoid enemy fire.

Trenches were built in zigzag patterns, which were easier to defend than straight lines.

DEFENSIVE ENGINEERING

Castles and forts were once built as safe havens against attacks, usually on top of hills so the occupants could see the surrounding area for many miles. For thousands of years, defensive walls surrounded settlements to block entry by enemies.

As weapons improved, engineering had to evolve to keep up. Walls were built with slit windows from which arrows could be fired, and ceilings often featured "murder holes" through which stones or hot liquids could be thrown. In the 14th century, the invention of cannons meant that castle and town walls had to be thickened to protect against cannon blasts. The use of explosives and, later, aircraft meant that castles and forts were no longer useful.

During many wars, trenches were dug to protect soldiers and prevent the advance of opposing armies. By the First World War, however, explosives had developed to a point that trenches were difficult to defend, and many soldiers died because of this outdated method.

THE MAGINOT LINE

Border of France and Germany

During the 1930s, growing tensions in Europe meant that many countries began preparing for war. In France, a 280-mile/450-kilometer line of small forts, tunnels, and large guns, known as the Maginot Line, was built along the border with Germany. However, this incredible feat of engineering stopped at the border between France and Belgium, so when the German army invaded France in 1940, they simply went around the Maginot Line by going through Belgium.

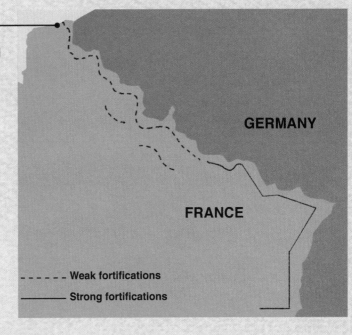

The Maginot Line had its own self-contained telephone and radio communication system.

GERMANY

FRANCE

- - - - - Weak fortifications
———— Strong fortifications

KRAK DES CHEVALIERS

Talkalakh District, Syria

Between 1096 and 1291, there was a series of religious wars between Christians and Muslims, known as the Crusades. Christian armies built castles to protect the lands that they controlled. One of these castles was the Krak des Chevaliers, which is located in modern-day Syria. Crusaders took control of the fortress in 1140 and made extensive fortifications. The castle had double 10-foot-/3-meter-thick walls and was so difficult to attack that it kept Muslim armies at bay for over 100 years.

The fortress could accommodate 2,000 soldiers, 1,000 horses, and supplies for up to five years.

GREAT WALL OF CHINA
Dandong to Lop Nur, China

The Great Wall of China is perhaps the greatest piece of defensive engineering in history. The first sections were built as early as 700 BCE, and others were added and connected over hundreds of years. Today, only parts of the wall remain, with much of it having disappeared over the centuries. The oldest sections have been destroyed due to erosion and people taking the bricks to use for other building projects, or for mining. The majority of the surviving wall was built in the Ming Dynasty, between the 14th and 17th centuries. Because it covered such a huge distance, materials used in different parts of the wall vary depending on what was available in the local area at the time—a mix of stone, bricks, mud, and wood.

At 13,050 miles/21,000 kilometers long, it is the longest structure humans have ever built. Only 8,700 miles/14,000 kilometers still stand today.

The average height of the wall is 23 feet/7 meters. At its highest, it is 46 feet/ 14 meters tall.

It is estimated that 400,000 people died building the wall, known as "the longest cemetery in the world."

Parts of the wall were restored for tourism in the 1950s.

The wall was built by soldiers, convicts, and peasants who were forced into labor.

THERE IS A POPULAR MYTH THAT THE GREAT WALL CAN BE SEEN FROM SPACE, BUT THIS IS UNTRUE.

The wall has around 7,000 lookout towers, placed 1–3 miles/ 2–5 kilometers apart.

It is believed that millions of people were involved in the building of the Great Wall.

ARTIFICIAL ISLANDS

People all over the world have been creating new islands for over 5,000 years. Some ancient artificial islands were built for defensive or religious reasons. Modern human-made islands are still being created for defense, but also to make extra space for growing cities. Island building can attract tourists and create jobs. However, the construction of some modern islands can be very expensive and harm the environment.

CRANNOG, SCOTLAND

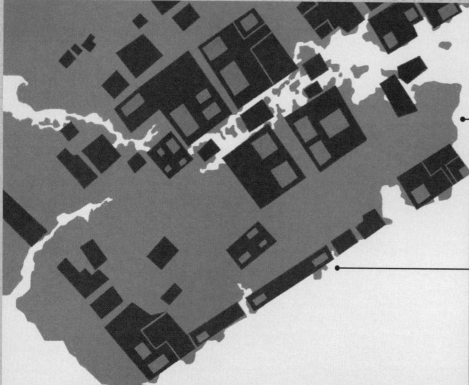

Nan Madol is sometimes called the Venice of the Pacific due to the network of canals that connect the islands.

Many historians believe that Nan Madol was built as a religious site where priests lived and worked.

NAN MADOL

Pohnpei, Micronesia

Next to the island of Pohnpei in the Pacific Ocean is a series of 92 ancient artificial islands known as Nan Madol. These islands stretch out along the coast with temples, palaces, and public baths built throughout. Very little is known about when and how these islands were constructed, but it is believed they were built about 900 years ago using huge volcanic rocks from the other side of Pohnpei. Nobody is sure how the rocks were transported or how they were placed in position in the ocean.

NAN MADOL, POHNPEI, MICRONESIA

BUILDING NEW ISLANDS

Some artificial islands are created by accident. The construction of dams and reservoirs causes water levels to rise, flooding areas of land. Any land that remains above the new water level becomes an island.

Early artificial islands from the Neolithic era, called crannogs, have been found in Scotland. The techniques used to build new islands have not changed much in millennia. Rocks and sand are built up from the floor of the lake or ocean, eventually rising out of the water and forming an island. This method works well when building small islands in calm water. However, many massive island building projects come with extra difficulties that have to be solved. The floor of the ocean or lake might not be strong enough to support a new island, so it will need to be leveled off with the addition of a concrete foundation before the construction starts.

Newly built islands in the ocean also have to be protected from severe weather, tides, and strong waves, which can cause damage. Concrete sea walls are sometimes added to stop this from happening, and constant maintenance is required to prevent the islands from being damaged by erosion.

CHUBU CENTRAIR AIRPORT

Nagoya, Japan

Many major cities along the ocean have built airports on artificial islands. This means that the airport can be close to the city center, and aircraft can take off and land without needing to avoid buildings. Japan's Chubu Centrair International Airport was built on an artificial island near the city of Nagoya. Over 10 million passengers pass through the airport every year.

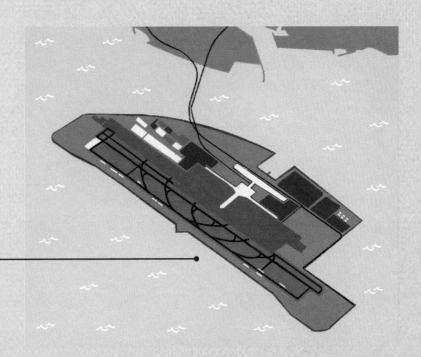

Chubu Centrair is one of four airports built on artificial islands in Japan.

Oil is extracted from below the ocean floor and transported to shore using an underwater pipeline.

NORTHSTAR ISLAND

Arctic Ocean

Six miles/10 kilometers north of Alaska in the Arctic Ocean is Northstar Island. It was constructed in order to drill for the oil that lies beneath the ocean floor. It was built in 2000 and is made of huge quantities of gravel, topped with thick slabs of concrete.

PALM JUMEIRAH
Dubai, United Arab Emirates

Off the coast of Dubai is the world's biggest artificial island, Palm Jumeirah. When viewed from the air, it looks like a palm tree. It was supposed to be one of three islands built next to each other, but only Palm Jumeirah has been completed so far, as the other two have been put on hold due to the high cost of construction. Work on Palm Jumeirah began in 2001 and was completed five years later. The base of the island is made from rocks blasted out from the nearby Hajar Mountains, while the top of the island is made from sand brought up from the seabed. The round exterior of the island is a breakwater and is there to protect the island from the ocean.

The 4 billion cubic feet/ 120 million cubic meters of sand dredged from the ocean floor to build Palm Jumeirah could make a 7-foot-/2-meter-wide wall that would circle the Earth three times.

The breakwater has two 328-foot/100-meter openings on either side to allow water to circulate properly.

NO CONCRETE OR STEEL WAS USED IN THE ISLAND. INSTEAD, BUILDERS CHOSE TO USE NATURAL ROCK AND SAND.

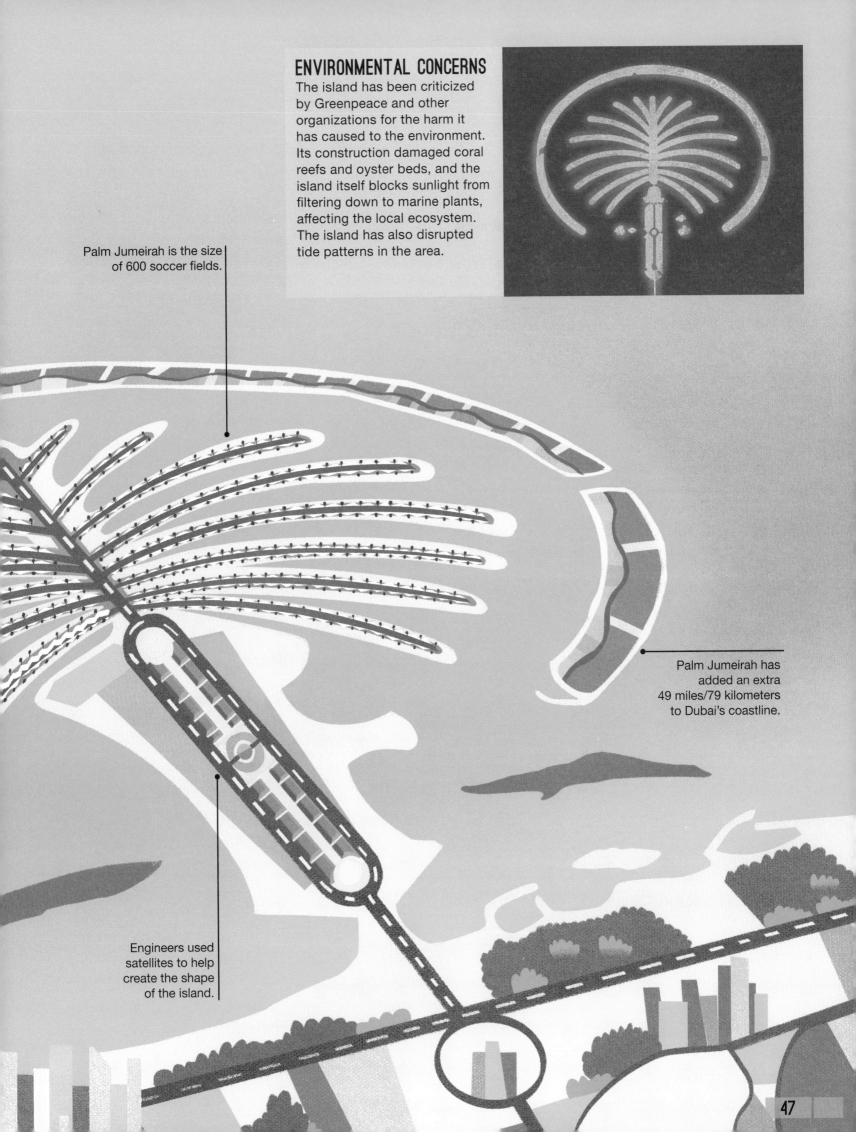

ENVIRONMENTAL CONCERNS

The island has been criticized by Greenpeace and other organizations for the harm it has caused to the environment. Its construction damaged coral reefs and oyster beds, and the island itself blocks sunlight from filtering down to marine plants, affecting the local ecosystem. The island has also disrupted tide patterns in the area.

Palm Jumeirah is the size of 600 soccer fields.

Palm Jumeirah has added an extra 49 miles/79 kilometers to Dubai's coastline.

Engineers used satellites to help create the shape of the island.

STATUES

Statues can be found in nearly every country in the world and have been created by civilizations for thousands of years. The oldest surviving statue in the world is the Lion Man of the Hohlenstein-Stadel in Germany, a 40,000-year-old figure that measures 12 inches/30 centimeters tall and is crafted from mammoth ivory. Statues are made for all sorts of reasons, but they are usually created to celebrate or remember something important and can include religious structures, monuments to great rulers or warriors, and memorials to those killed in wars.

LION MAN OF THE HOHLENSTEIN-STADEL, GERMANY

MOAI

Rapa Nui, South Pacific

The remote Rapa Nui, or Easter Island, is most famous for its ancient stonework, particularly the 887 carved statues known as moai. Estimated to have been carved anywhere between 1100 and 1680 from volcanic rock, each statue is believed to represent a deceased leader. The figures were carved before they were transported to their final location, and there are many theories on how this was done. Some believe that the statues were pulled on large wooden sleds, while others think that they were secured with ropes and "walked" there by a team of people.

The figures are often known as Easter Island heads, as many were discovered buried up to their necks.

Builders did not have metal tools so they carved the soft volcanic rock with harder stone tools.

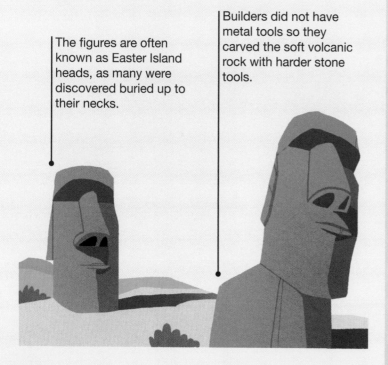

Ancient monks believed that the giant Buddha would help calm the turbulent waters of nearby rivers.

233 feet/71 meters

LESHAN GIANT BUDDHA

Sichuan Province, China

This huge statue is a monolith, carved from a single piece of stone in the side of a cliff. It was built between 713 and 803 CE and is over 230 feet/70 meters tall. It is the largest stone Buddha in the world and was also the largest statue in the world for many centuries.

THE KELPIES

Falkirk, Scotland

Kelpies are mythical spirits that live in water and can take on the shape of a human or horse. These giant statues of horse-headed kelpies were created in 2013 and form a gateway to the newest part of the Forth and Clyde Canal. The statues are made from hundreds of hand-cut sheets of steel and were welded together using the same techniques used by local shipbuilders.

The Kelpies' designer, Andy Scott, created a 10-foot/3-meter model of the statues, which he scanned with lasers to help sculptors create the full-sized models.

98 feet/30 meters

STATUE OF UNITY

Gujarat, India

The largest statue in the world is currently in India. The Statue of Unity celebrates the life of Sardar Patel, one of the leaders of India's independence movement. Construction of the statue started in 2014 and was completed four years later. It is 597 feet/182 meters tall and is made of large bronze panels. India did not have a factory that could make the panels, so they were made in China and then shipped to India.

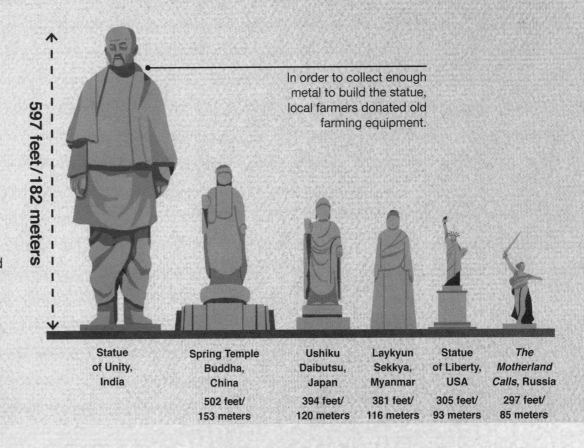

In order to collect enough metal to build the statue, local farmers donated old farming equipment.

597 feet/182 meters

Statue of Unity, India	Spring Temple Buddha, China	Ushiku Daibutsu, Japan	Laykyun Sekkya, Myanmar	Statue of Liberty, USA	*The Motherland Calls*, Russia
	502 feet/ 153 meters	394 feet/ 120 meters	381 feet/ 116 meters	305 feet/ 93 meters	297 feet/ 85 meters

BUILDING STATUES

Whether they are built for religious, political, or decorative reasons, statues are intended to be seen by as many people as possible, so they are usually very large and erected in public places.

Smaller statues tend to be made from just one piece of material, such as a single block of stone or a single sheet of metal. Bigger statues require more materials and are usually made in much smaller sections that are then slotted together like a jigsaw puzzle.

Engineering skills are crucial in the construction of statues. It's important to understand how each material can actually be used.

Creating and putting together all of the separate pieces of a large statue takes careful calculation and planning.

Many statues are made from materials that are not available locally. This means that the statues are constructed where the materials are available and then brought to the place where they will stand or that the materials are imported before the statue is built.

STATUE OF LIBERTY
New York City, USA

In New York Harbor is the small Liberty Island. On it stands one of the most famous statues in the world. The Statue of Liberty was a gift from the people of France to the United States of America, sculpted by Frédéric Auguste Bartholdi, to celebrate the centennial of American independence from Britain. Work began on the copper statue in 1875. Separate pieces were built in France and then transported by ship to the USA, where they were put together. This was a long process, and the statue was not completed until 1886.

GREEN LADY

Though the statue is known for its distinctive shade of green, it was not always this color. Originally, it was bronze-colored, but when left outside, a process called oxidization caused the copper to develop a green patina on its surface. This has not been cleaned off because it helps protect the statue from the weather.

The statue itself is 151 feet/46 meters tall. Including its plinth, it stands at 305 feet/93 meters high.

The seven spikes of the statue's crown represent the seven oceans and continents, symbolizing world freedom.

Lady Liberty holds a tablet inscribed with the date the USA declared independence—July 4, 1776.

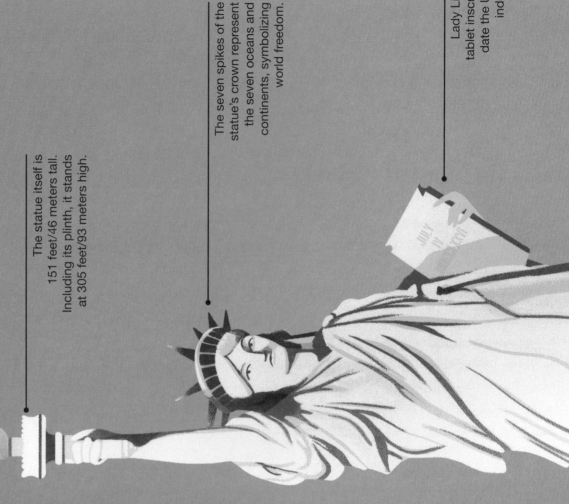

VISITORS CAN GET TO THE CROWN OF THE STATUE BY CLIMBING UP A SPIRAL STAIRCASE OF 146 STEPS.

The statue is made of 300 copper sheets. Each sheet is about 2 millimeters thick.

In high winds, the statue can safely sway about 3 inches/8 centimeters without falling over or getting damaged.

ENGINEERING MYSTERIES

Though historians and engineers have studied our world's ancient engineering marvels closely, and have learned much about them, there are some incredible structures that are still a mystery to us. Many early civilizations didn't have a writing system of any kind, so they didn't leave many clues about why they built what they did. It is often unknown how ancient people built these huge, elaborate structures without the modern tools, materials, and equipment we have today.

PUMAPUNKU

Tiwanaku, Bolivia

Nobody is sure when this Bolivian temple was built, although most people think it was around 600 CE. Many of the huge blocks of stone used to build the complex came from over 6 miles/10 kilometers away, and there are no indications of how the stone was transported to the building site. The stones themselves fit together so perfectly that not even a sheet of paper can be inserted between them—to this day, nobody knows how this engineering marvel was achieved.

Many of the stones are held together with copper fasteners, which may have been poured between the stones while molten.

STONE SPHERES

Palmar Sur, Costa Rica

During the 1930s, workers clearing part of the Costa Rican jungle discovered a vast area filled with hundreds of carved stone spheres. These mysterious spheres, known as Las Bolas or the Diquís Spheres, ranged from a few centimeters to over 7 feet/ 2 meters in diameter. Nobody knows how old the spheres are, which civilization created them, or why they were made in the first place.

The people who made the stones may have heated them to make them easier to carve.

When the spheres were found in the 1930s, workers drilled holes in some of them, looking for gold, but found nothing.

PLAIN OF JARS

Xiangkhoang Plateau, Laos

Thousands of huge stone jars, built between 500 BCE and 500 CE, can be found in an open plain in Laos. Though nobody knows for sure why these were made, human remains have been found in some, leading archaeologists to believe they may have been used for burial practices. One jar has a "frogman" carved on the lid—similar carvings have been found in China from around the same time.

LAOTIAN LEGEND TELLS OF A RACE OF GIANTS WHO BUILT THE JARS TO STORE WINE.

Few lids have been found, suggesting they were made from perishable materials, such as wood.

ANTIKYTHERA MECHANISM

Antikythera, Greece

In 1901, a diver discovered a lump of ancient bronze and wood at the bottom of the sea. Scientists were amazed to find it was a clockwork machine from about 100 BCE. It may have been used to track the stars and planets and work out the dates of future eclipses of the sun. Although there is no doubt it comes from ancient Greece, no similar machine has ever been found, so how such a complex device was built remains a question that archaeologists are seeking to answer.

The mechanism contains 37 interlocking gears.

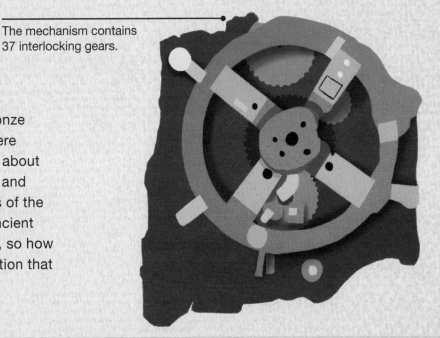

UNANSWERED QUESTIONS

Today, it is possible to build and engineer projects from lots of different materials. It does not matter if the materials needed are found nearby, as they can be transported from anywhere in the world. However, many ancient structures use materials that came from far away, and experts can't always agree on how they would have been transported.

Even once the materials arrived, there are more questions to be answered. Societies (such as the Mayan people, page 8) that had yet to implement metal tools used rudimentary stone and wooden tools to build amazing and complex structures, leaving no clues behind about how they did it.

STONEHENGE
Wiltshire, England

Stonehenge is a prehistoric ring of standing stones that was built between 3000 and 2000 BCE, one of the most famous ancient monuments in the world. There were two kinds of stone used in the structure. The larger sarsen stones weigh about 28 tons/25 metric tons and were brought from a site about 15 miles/24 kilometers away. The smaller bluestones weigh about 4 tons/3 metric tons and come from a site in Wales—180 miles/290 kilometers away. Nobody knows how the stones were transported to Stonehenge over such a long distance. Once they arrived on site, workers raised the stones by pushing them into a hole and pulling them upright with ropes.

Over time, many of the stones have fallen down. In 1901, 1958, and 1964, several stones were lifted up and put back into place.

Stonehenge was built in several stages, with the famous stone circle added 500 years after the first burial mounds were made.

In 2013, archaeologists found the cremated remains of about fifty-eight skeletons, suggesting Stonehenge may have been built for burial purposes.

STRANGE STRUCTURE

Stonehenge is made up of an outer circle of 30 larger sarsen stones. This circle surrounds a horseshoe formed from five large stone arches and two smaller bluestone circles. The whole structure is surrounded by a ditch. There is also a circle of small holes inside Stonehenge called the Aubrey holes. The significance of these holes remains a mystery.

The giant arches made of three stones are known as trilithons.

Nobody is sure of Stonehenge's original purpose, but most people agree that it was created for religious reasons.

ONE LEGEND CLAIMS THAT STONEHENGE WAS ORIGINALLY BUILT IN IRELAND AND TRANSPORTED TO ENGLAND BY THE WIZARD MERLIN.

When struck, the sarsen stones make a strange ringing sound. This seemingly magical property might explain why they were painstakingly brought from so far away.

Large quantities of flakes from the sarsen and bluestone were found in a field near Stonehenge, which indicates that the stones were shaped after being transported there.

COMMEMORATIVE ENGINEERING

The monuments and structures left behind by past civilizations provide some intriguing clues as to their culture and history. While most works of engineering serve a practical purpose, some are built to commemorate important people and events. From wars won and lost to great tragedies and sporting events, these structures stand as reminders of important moments in history for future generations.

ARCELORMITTAL ORBIT, LONDON, ENGLAND

PLACE DE LA BASTILLE

Paris, France

Towards the end of the 18th century, France was in the midst of a revolution as ordinary people fought to overthrow their aristocratic rulers. A key turning point in the French Revolution was the storming of the Bastille (a political prison in the center of Paris), which was seen as a symbol of tyranny. To commemorate this event and celebrate their freedom, the French people built a large square on the site of the Bastille, called Place de la Bastille.

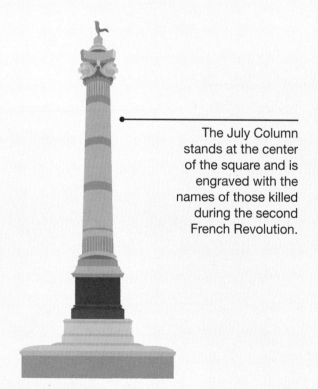

The July Column stands at the center of the square and is engraved with the names of those killed during the second French Revolution.

The large, strong panes of glass known as sheet glass used in the palace had only recently been developed at the time.

The original design for the palace was scribbled on blotting paper and can be found in the Victoria and Albert Museum in London.

CRYSTAL PALACE

London, England

In 1851, London hosted the Great Exhibition, celebrating works of industry and culture from all over the world. Famous people, including Charles Darwin, Charlotte Brontë, and Queen Victoria, visited it. To house the exhibition, the Crystal Palace was built. This 1,847-foot-/563-meter-long glass building was originally located in Hyde Park. It was later relocated to another area of London—Sydenham Hill—where it remained until it was destroyed by a fire in 1936. The area was renamed Crystal Palace in commemoration of the extraordinary monument.

BUILDING TO REMEMBER

There are many different reasons for commemorative engineering. In the wake of the First and Second World Wars, millions were dead, and entire nations were in mourning. To honor those killed and acknowledge the horrors of war, towns, cities, and countries built war memorials.

Memorials are also built for positive occasions. Many countries have built huge monuments and statues to celebrate their independence from foreign rule, such as the Independence Monument in Cambodia, which was built to celebrate the country's freedom from French rule. Statues have been built when a city hosts a major world event, such as the Olympics or a World Fair. The sculpture ArcelorMittal Orbit was designed to commemorate the London 2012 Olympics. Not only a chance to show off to visitors, these monuments serve as a reminder of the event in the years that follow.

WARSAW UPRISING MONUMENT

Warsaw, Poland

Following a Polish uprising against Nazi occupation in 1944, during which thousands of people were killed and 90 percent of the capital city, Warsaw, was destroyed, the Polish people erected the Warsaw Uprising Monument. The 33-foot/10-meter bronze statue depicts insurgents in combat by a collapsed building and a rebel climbing into a manhole—this is a reference to the way the Polish Resistance used the city's sewer system to smuggle people and information.

The monument is really two separate sculptures: one made from bronze and one made from stone.

Almost the entire Old Town neighborhood of Warsaw, where the monument is situated, was destroyed in the uprising and then rebuilt.

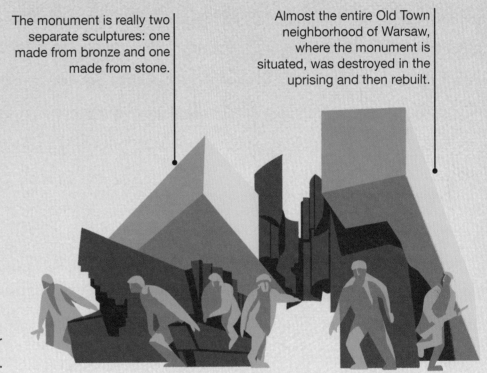

One sculpture found at the monument, *Unearthed*, is based on facial reconstructions of three skeletons found at the site.

It is hard to say how many people were buried at the cemetery, but it was likely close to 15,000.

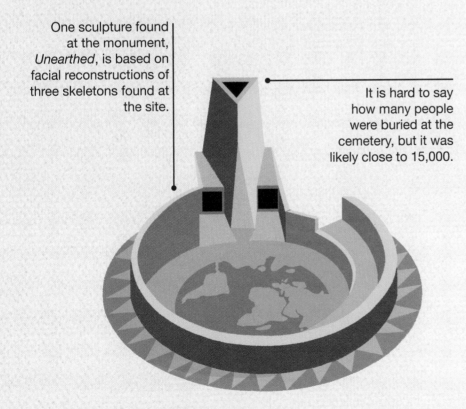

AFRICAN BURIAL GROUND NATIONAL MONUMENT

New York City, USA

Built on the site of the biggest colonial-era African American cemetery in the USA, the African Burial Ground National Monument in New York commemorates those who died under slavery. It serves as a reminder of the major role that slavery played in building New York. The memorial consists of several pieces of art and a stone map, named Circle of Diaspora, meant to honor the millions who were taken and lost in the transatlantic slave trade and to celebrate the diversity of the African diaspora.

EIFFEL TOWER

Paris, France

The Eiffel Tower in Paris is one of the best-known pieces of commemorative engineering in the world. It was built between 1887 and 1889 as the entrance to the 1889 World Fair. Standing at 1,063 feet/324 meters tall, it was the highest structure in the world for 41 years. The tower was named after the engineer who built it, Gustave Eiffel, who also worked on an early conception of the Panama Canal (pages 30–31) and the Statue of Liberty (pages 50–51). The tower was first built as a temporary structure only intended to last 20 years, but later found a new life as a radio transmitter. Today, the Eiffel Tower is one of the most visited tourist attractions in the world, with more than seven million people flocking to see it every year.

LONG WAY UP

While it is possible to climb the 1,665 steps to the top of the Eiffel Tower, most people choose to take the elevator. There are two elevators in the tower, which travel a combined distance of 64,000 miles/103,000 kilometers every year—the equivalent of two and a half trips around the world.

Seventy-two engineers worked on the construction of the Eiffel Tower. Their names are engraved into the metal on one side of the tower.

1,063 feet/324 meters

18,038 METAL PARTS WERE USED IN THE BUILDING OF THE TOWER, ALONG WITH 2.5 MILLION RIVETS.

Today, the tower is built to last. It can safely sway up to 3½ inches/9 centimeters in high winds.

When the tower was being built, a group of French artists and writers objected to the tower. They called it the "useless and monstrous Eiffel Tower."

COPYCATS
There are a number of replicas of this iconic tower around the world, including in Las Vegas and Tokyo. The town of Paris, Texas, has a smaller copy of the Eiffel Tower with a cowboy hat perched on top.

The tower is painted by hand every seven years to prevent it from rusting.

BUILDING FOR EARTHQUAKES

Earth's crust is made up of huge tectonic plates. Sometimes, these crash into each other, causing earthquakes. Some of the biggest cities in the world, such as San Francisco, Tokyo, Manila, and Istanbul are built on the joins between tectonic plates, called fault lines, where earthquakes are most common. These areas can be subject to massive damage and loss of life. Engineers are tasked to build structures that can withstand earthquakes.

101 SKYSCRAPER

The 101 skyscraper was the tallest building in the world until the construction of the Burj Khalifa in 2010 (pages 16–17). To prevent earthquake damage, it has the world's largest and heaviest tuned mass damper (see opposite). This giant steel sphere is suspended between the 92nd and 87th floors.

In 2015, a storm caused the huge damper to sway by 3 feet/1 meter— but the tower stayed standing.

1,667 feet/508 meters

AKASHI KAIKYŌ BRIDGE

Kobe to Awaji Island, Japan

Japan is in part of the world known as the ring of fire, where earthquakes and volcanic eruptions are common, and so earthquake engineering is very important there. The Akashi Kaikyō suspension bridge over the Akashi Strait is nearly 13,000 feet/4,000 meters long. Tuned mass dampers inside the supporting towers help protect the bridge from earthquakes.

The Akashi Kaikyō Bridge is the strongest, longest, and most expensive suspension bridge in the world.

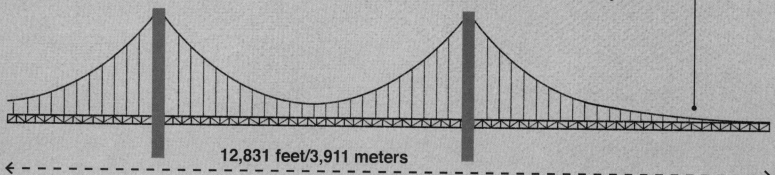

12,831 feet/3,911 meters

PREVENTING DAMAGE

One of the most common ways to make any structure earthquake-proof is to use materials that are flexible, such as wood and steel. Rigid materials, like stone, cannot move around as much, making the structure more likely to collapse during an earthquake. Tall buildings can also sway around more easily. This is one of the reasons why cities commonly hit by earthquakes have tall buildings.

Extra steel beams can provide buildings with added protection. These help to control the way the building moves during an earthquake. The beams allow the bottom of the building more movement, which keeps the upper portion of the structure from toppling over.

The design of a building's foundation is also important in earthquake engineering. Buildings and bridges can be built with foundations that sway from side to side so that the building can remain stable during an earthquake.

Some buildings and bridges have a heavy device made of concrete or steel, called a tuned mass damper, built into them. During an earthquake, a tuned mass damper will compensate for the structure's movement to help maintain balance and keep the building from collapsing.

MARMARAY TUNNEL

Istanbul, Turkey

Because tunnels are deep underground, they are usually less damaged by earthquakes. Sometimes, though, the shaking ground causes soil to behave like a liquid (a process known as liquefaction), and tunnels can float to the surface. When the Marmaray Tunnel was built under Istanbul between 2004 and 2013, workers made the soil outside the tunnel denser by adding liquid concrete to it. This reduced the danger of liquefaction.

ADDITIONAL STEEL BEAMS

LOS ANGELES CITY HALL

Los Angeles, USA

Following damage by several major earthquakes, Los Angeles city officials decided to renovate the city hall to make it earthquake-proof. Improving old buildings in this way is called a seismic retrofit. In 2001, the foundations of Los Angeles City Hall were changed so that, during an earthquake, they would move, keeping the rest of the building still.

The hall's tower was badly cracked by an earthquake in 1971.

The retrofit involved adding thousands of tons of steel and concrete to the building.

TOKYO SKYTREE

Tokyo, Japan

Tokyo's tallest structure, the 2,080-foot/634-meter Tokyo Skytree, is an incredible piece of earthquake engineering. The main structure consists of strong steel tubes and has a massive concrete column that runs down the middle of the building. This column sits on six giant rubber bearings. The steel tubes and concrete column are completely separate and move in different directions from one another. This creates a counterbalance, much like a tuned mass damper, and stops the tower from collapsing in an earthquake.

Tokyo Skytree is the tallest tower in the world and the second tallest structure after the Burj Khalifa.

The concrete column is just over 1,230 feet/375 meters tall.

PAGODAS ALSO USE A CENTRAL COLUMN TO PROTECT THEM FROM EARTHQUAKES. THESE COLUMNS ARE CALLED SHINBASHIRA.

2,080 feet/634 meters tall

The design of Tokyo Skytree is based on traditional Japanese pagodas (a type of tower).

Tokyo Skytree is painted a bluish-white shade called Skytree White. It is based on a traditional Japanese color called aijiro.

MEMORABLE HEIGHT

The tower's 2,080-foot/634-meter height was chosen very specifically. The region where Tokyo Skytree stands was once called Mushashi, and, in Japanese, the numbers 6, 3, and 4 are pronounced "mu," "sha," and "shi."

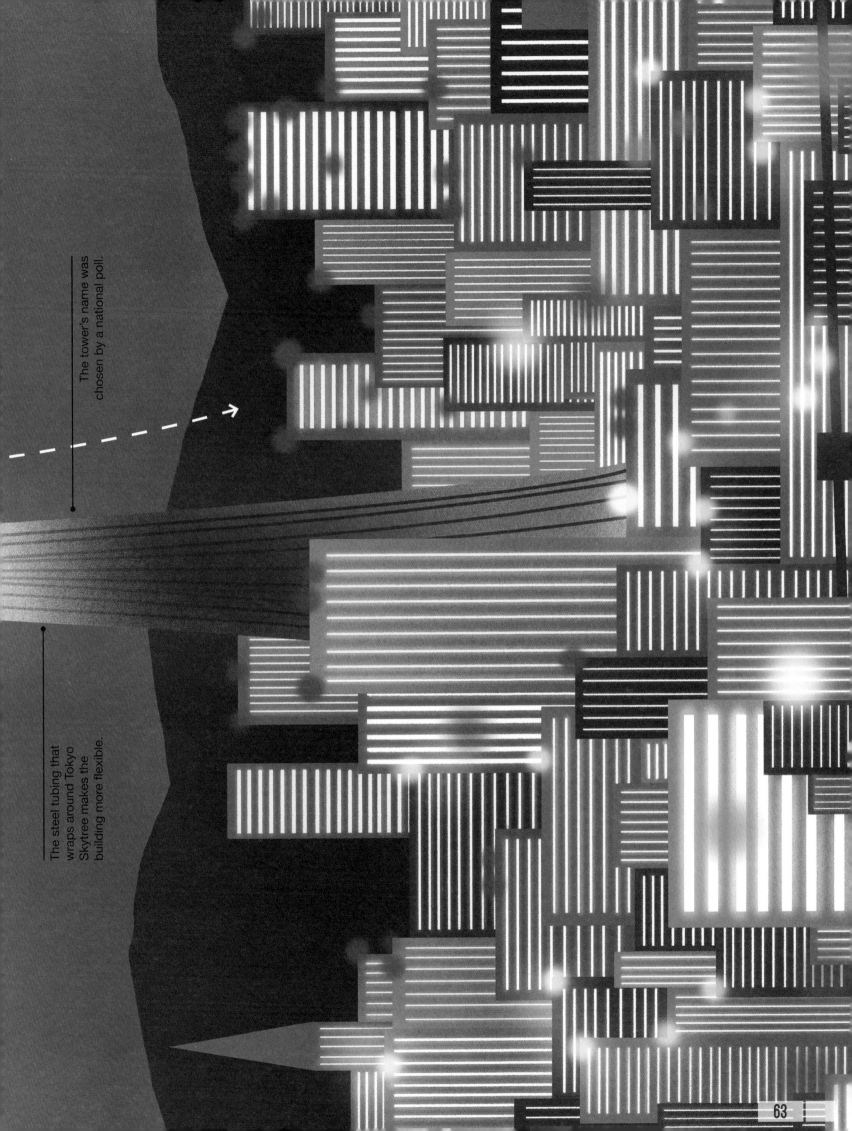

The tower's name was chosen by a national poll.

The steel tubing that wraps around Tokyo Skytree makes the building more flexible.

MARINE ENGINEERING

Water covers over 70 percent of the Earth's surface. We rely on oceans to transport people and goods around the globe. Thirty percent of all the oil and gas that we use comes from under the ocean, and an increasing amount of renewable energy comes from offshore wind turbines and tidal barrages (pages 32–33).

A PAINTED DISC FROM AROUND 5000 BCE FOUND IN KUWAIT SHOWS THE EARLIEST KNOWN DEPICTION OF A SHIP.

MOSE PROJECT

Venice, Italy

The ancient city of Venice in Italy is one of the most recognizable places in the world. Flooding has occurred in Venice for centuries, but climate change means that these floods are going to get bigger and more frequent, causing more damage. The MOSE project is a giant flood defense engineering project to protect the city and one of the largest engineering projects in the world. Work started in 2003.

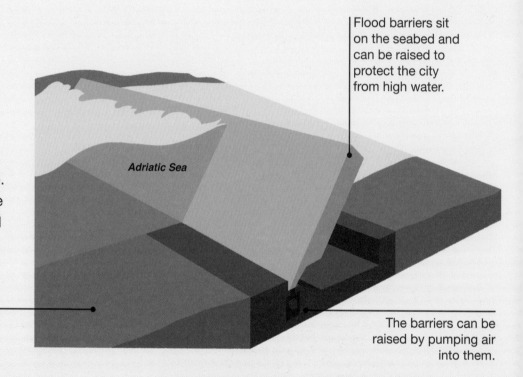

Flood barriers sit on the seabed and can be raised to protect the city from high water.

Adriatic Sea

The flood barriers weigh around 330 tons/300 metric tons.

The barriers can be raised by pumping air into them.

SEAWISE GIANT

The longest ship ever built was *Seawise Giant*. Built in 1979, it was about 1,500 feet/460 meters long and was used to transport oil around the world. It was so enormous that it couldn't fit through the English Channel or the Suez or Panama Canals (pages 30–31). It was sunk in 1988 during the Gulf War but was later raised and restored. It was finally scrapped in 2009.

1,453 feet/443 meters long

1,503 feet/458 meters long

This enormous ship was 50 feet/ 15 meters longer than the Empire State building.

PLONGEUR

The first submarine to be powered by engines was built in France in 1863. It was called *Plongeur* (meaning "diver" in French) and was 148 feet/45 meters long. *Plongeur* had a top speed of 4 miles/7 kilometers per hour and could dive to a depth of 33 feet/10 meters. Its engine was powered using 23 tanks of compressed air, which took up most of the space inside.

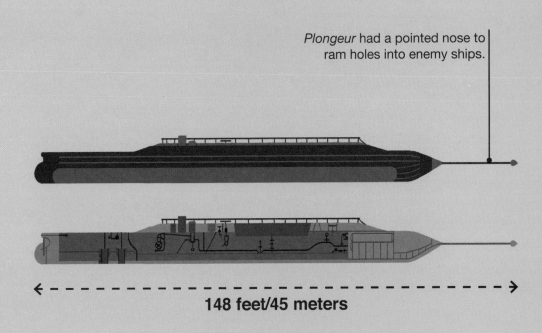

Plongeur had a pointed nose to ram holes into enemy ships.

148 feet/45 meters

PETRONIUS

Gulf of Mexico, Atlantic Ocean

Petronius is an oil platform in the Gulf of Mexico, 130 miles/210 kilometers south of New Orleans, Louisiana. Until the building of the Burj Khalifa (pages 16–17), it was the tallest structure in the world, measuring just under 2,000 feet/610 meters. However, most of it is underwater, with only 246 feet/75 meters emerging above the water. It is designed to sway in high winds, to prevent it from being damaged by extreme weather.

246 feet/75 meters above water

In 2004, Petronius was badly damaged by Hurricane Ivan, but it was repaired within a year.

NAVAL ARCHITECTURE

Some marine engineers, known as naval architects, use their engineering skills to build and maintain ships and submarines. When starting a new project, they must first decide on the shape and size of a ship, as this will determine how quickly and easily it can move through water and affect its stability in high winds and strong waves. Naval architects are also part of the design and maintenance team for oil and gas platforms, wind turbines, and tidal barrages.

Engineering at sea is different from other kinds of engineering because naval architects have to understand how the sea behaves. Oceans are constantly moving and changing with the waves and tides and can become dangerous during storms. The salt in seawater also causes metal to rust quickly.

Rising temperatures caused by climate change mean sea levels are rising. Many major cities, like New York, Mumbai, and Shanghai, are located along a coast and are under increasing threat from flooding. Marine engineers are involved in designing and building new flood defenses to protect these cities.

SS GREAT EASTERN

Liverpool, England

Isambard Kingdom Brunel was one of the greatest engineers of the 19th century. He designed tunnels, bridges, railway lines, and ships, many of which can still be seen today. One of his greatest achievements was the ship SS *Great Eastern*. At 692 feet/211 meters long, it was by far the largest ship in the world when it was launched in 1858. It was originally meant to carry passengers from Britain to Australia, but ended up carrying people across the Atlantic Ocean instead. It was finally scrapped in 1899 after more than 40 years in service.

The ship was so big that it had to be built and launched sideways, as there were no docks big enough to hold it.

The ship ended its life as a floating concert hall, sailing up and down the River Mersey in Liverpool, England.

The top mast was rescued when the ship was scrapped and is now a flagpole at Anfield, the home of Liverpool Football Club.

THERE IS A STORY THAT TWO SKELETONS WERE FOUND BETWEEN THE DOUBLE HULLS, AND THIS WAS WHY THE *GREAT EASTERN* WAS SUPPOSEDLY CURSED.

DOUBLE HULL

One of SS *Great Eastern*'s engineering firsts was having two hulls—one inside the other. This was an added safety feature in case water got through the outside hull.

In 1864, SS *Great Eastern* was sold to a company that used it to lay telegraph cables under the ocean.

AGE OF EXPLORATION
As people began to explore further and seek out new lands, it became possible to transport goods and materials from all over the world on ships. For the first time, engineers and builders had a whole planet of resources to choose from.

HARNESSING ELECTRICITY
In the 19th century, engineers began discovering new ways to power machinery using electricity, leading to many developments that shape how we live today. Scientists Thomas Edison and Joseph Swan patented the light bulb, while Nikola Tesla and Guglielmo Marconi competed to be the first to invent the radio.

1400-1600

1800-1900

STATUE OF LIBERTY
1875

1858
SS *GREAT EASTERN*

1863
LONDON UNDERGROUND

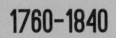

1760-1840

INDUSTRIAL REVOLUTION
The Industrial Revolution was a huge turning point for engineering. People moved from using hand tools to machines, and mass production became common. Suddenly, huge structures could be built far more quickly and with fewer workers. The steam engine was also developed around this time, allowing people to move materials more easily.

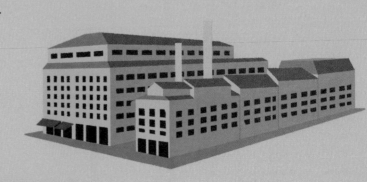

ENGINEERING TIME LINE

NEOLITHIC BUILDERS

As far back as 9000 BCE, humans were building homes, temples, and tombs. Skara Brae, in Scotland, was built around 3200 BCE and is so well-preserved that it has given archaeologists invaluable insight into Neolithic building techniques.

ROMAN ENGINEERS

One of the greatest achievements of Roman engineers was the invention of the aqueduct, which allowed them to bring water to their cities over great distances. This led to widespread use of water wheels, which powered mills and mining equipment using hydropower.

12000–3000 BCE

STONEHENGE
3000 BCE

GREAT SPHINX
2558 BCE

0

221 BCE
GREAT WALL OF CHINA

476 CE–**1500**

3000–300 BCE

EGYPTIAN BUILDERS

The skill of Egyptian engineers was phenomenal. Despite not having access to modern tools, they managed to build huge, extravagant palaces, temples, pyramids, and towns. They used a series of ramps, pulleys, and thousands of workers to haul heavy stones to the top of tall pyramids and even made their own bricks from clay.

MIDDLE AGES

During the Middle Ages, much of the world was at war. The Crusades raged in the Middle East, and many European countries fought against one another. Because of this, there were many advances in military engineering. Castles and fortresses were built for defense and weapons such as cannons and huge catapults, called trebuchets, were developed.

FAMOUS ENGINEERS

Our world would not be what it is today without engineers. Since human beings first evolved, pioneering men and women have shaped the way we live. From transport to buildings, weaponry to bridges, these magnificent engineers have changed the course of human history with their ingenious inventions.

THE FIRST WOMAN TO RECEIVE AN ENGINEERING DEGREE WAS ELIZABETH BRAGG IN 1876.

Imhotep's achievements were so great that later ancient Egyptians worshipped him as a god.

IMHOTEP

Egypt, approximately 2600 BCE

The first recorded engineer in history, Imhotep, supervised the building of the Pyramid of Djoser in Egypt. This pyramid, and others like it, are so well constructed that some people believe that aliens made them. The truth, however, is far more impressive. Using innovative techniques and new mathematics, ancient Egyptian engineers achieved this massive feat. Imhotep's buildings also included early examples of stone columns.

ARCHIMEDES

Greece, 287–212 BCE

Ancient Greek mathematician and engineer Archimedes invented all sorts of tools—including a device for raising water, known as the Archimedes' screw. He is perhaps most famous for discovering a way to calculate the volume of an object using water displacement while he was taking a bath. On discovering this, he reportedly leapt from the bath and ran down the street naked, shouting "Eureka!"

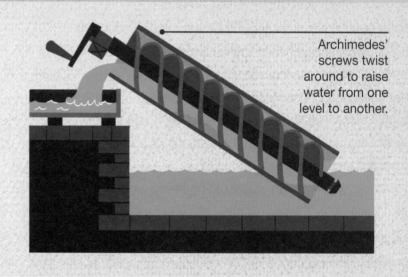

Archimedes' screws twist around to raise water from one level to another.

The wind spins the dial on an anemometer, which raises a piece of wood. The higher it is raised, the stronger the wind.

LEONARDO DA VINCI

Italy, 1452–1519

Leonardo da Vinci was known as a polymath—someone who has knowledge of many different areas. He was a world-renowned artist, writer, historian, mathematician, and engineer, among other things. One of da Vinci's obsessions was the anemometer, a machine designed by Leon Battista Alberti, which measured wind speed. Da Vinci spent many years altering and improving the original design.

EMILY ROEBLING

USA, 1843–1903

In 1869, engineer Washington Roebling was named chief engineer of the iconic Brooklyn Bridge in New York. However, after he became sick and unable to work, his wife Emily took over the role, planning and supervising the project. At a time when women were rarely allowed to attend universities and were barred from many careers, engineering included, Emily's brilliant work shone out.

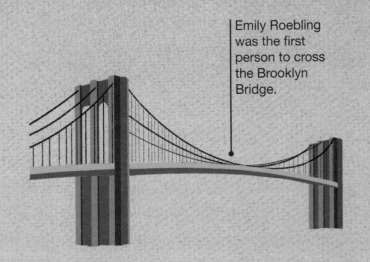

Emily Roebling was the first person to cross the Brooklyn Bridge.

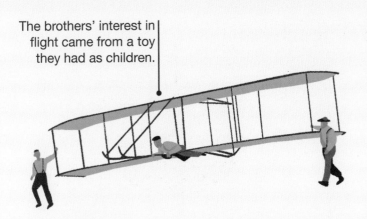

The brothers' interest in flight came from a toy they had as children.

WILBUR AND ORVILLE WRIGHT

USA, 1867–1912 and 1871–1948

The Wright brothers will go down in engineering history as the inventors of the airplane. On December 17, 1903, on a beach in North Carolina, their *Wright Flyer* took to the sky for the first time—for twelve seconds. This short flight changed the way humans traveled forever, and less than 50 years later, a human being traveled to space for the first time.

FAZLUR RAHMAN KHAN

Bangladesh/USA, 1929–1982

Fazlur Rahman Khan is a Bangladeshi-American architect and engineer who is often credited as the "father of the modern skyscraper" and the "Einstein of structural engineering." He created the tube principle, the basis of almost all tall buildings today. This meant building a strong frame of columns and beams around the perimeter of a tower. The tower then acts as a hollow cylinder helping the structure to better withstand earthquakes and high winds.

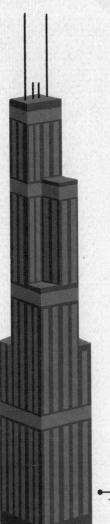

The Willis Tower in Chicago is one of Khan's best-known designs.

HEDY LAMARR

Austria/USA, 1914–2000

Hedy Lamarr's main claim to fame was her successful career as a Hollywood actress who appeared on the big screen all over the world. What many people may not know is that she was also a talented engineer and pioneered a new kind of radio signal for powering missiles during the Second World War. Many people believe this helped lead to the invention of Wi-Fi.

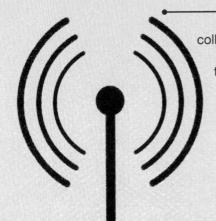

Lamarr and her collaborator developed spread spectrum technology that was used in naval operations for years.

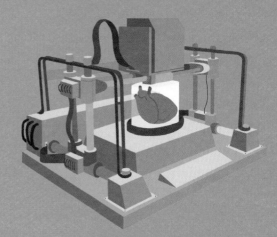

TWENTY-FIRST CENTURY

Even today, the world of engineering is changing rapidly. 3D printing has provided a way to create electrical parts, building materials, and even living tissues, while the Internet has allowed people to access information with a single tap. And still, people are trying to build higher, faster, stronger . . .

2001- PRESENT

GOLDEN GATE BRIDGE
1937

INTERNATIONAL SPACE STATION
1998

TOKYO SKYTREE
2012

2006
PALM JUMEIRAH

2012
THE SHARD

1957-1969

SPACE RACE

This era saw some incredible engineering breakthroughs as the USA and the USSR competed to be the first to make it to space. Only a few decades after the first plane was developed, we were developing ways to send animals and people into zero gravity. The first satellite was the Russian Sputnik, the first person in space was Yuri Gagarin, and, in 1969, two American astronauts set foot on the moon.

TODAY, A LOT OF ENGINEERING IS FOCUSED ON MAKING THE WORLD A BETTER PLACE WITH REUSABLE FUELS, CLEAN WATER, AND MEDICAL BREAKTHROUGHS.

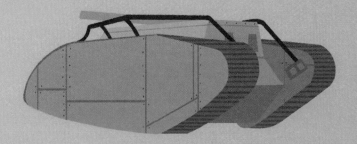

TECHNOCRACY

Following the First World War, some people in the USA and Canada started calling for technocracy—replacing politicians and business people with scientists and engineers. Though this never came to pass, it showed how valued the work of engineers was in the 20th century.

FIRST WORLD WAR

The invention of the tank changed the way people fought wars. Soldiers could travel across dangerous ground with a lower risk of being shot, and armies could seize more land in one go with fewer fatalities. Other military advancements, including poison gas and fighter planes, were also developed at this time.

1930

EIFFEL TOWER
1889

1914-1918

HOOVER DAM
1936

1914
PANAMA CANAL

1916
TRANS-SIBERIAN RAILWAY

1900-2000

TWENTIETH CENTURY

The 20th century saw a host of engineering breakthroughs. The invention of cars and planes allowed the movement of people and goods more quickly and easily than ever. The birth of computers meant that engineers could do calculations, run simulations, and design new structures efficiently.

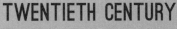

THE FUTURE

For centuries, engineers have come up with practical solutions to the problems they face in the world they live in. They have developed new tools, materials, and techniques to make building new structures easier and more practical. Even today, new problems are presenting themselves for engineers to overcome.

PROSTHETIC ARM

GREEN ENGINEERING

The construction of new railways, bridges, and buildings all create dangerous greenhouse gases. For instance, the making of concrete—an important material in most buildings—is one of the biggest sources of carbon dioxide. In addition, most cars, trains, and planes run on fossil fuels, which are damaging to the environment, so engineers must look for new, renewable forms of energy. Huge wind turbines can convert wind to energy, and engineers are finding new ways to produce energy from sunlight, water, plants, and even the force of the tides (pages 32–33). Some green engineers are trying to incorporate oxygen production into human-made structures, such as Bosco Verticale in Milan, Italy.

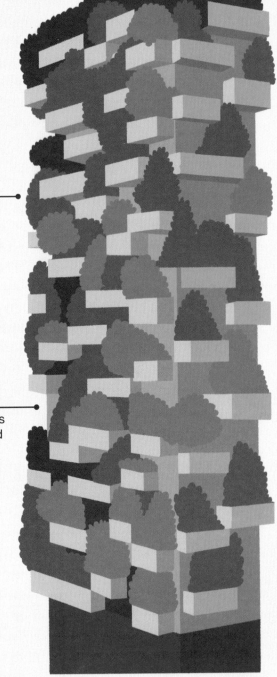

Bosco Verticale, or Vertical Forest, in Milan, Italy, helps to produce oxygen and prevent smog.

The two towers contain around 17,000 plants each.

Many coastal towns have flood walls to protect them from rising waters.

CHANGING WEATHER

Global warming is causing major changes in the planet's weather, which will only continue to get worse in the future. Engineers must work to find new ways to make sure that our towns and cities are protected from extreme weather and natural disasters, such as hurricanes, wildfires, and flooding.

SMARTPHONES

Today, billions of people carry smartphones, which allow us to be far more connected than any other generation before us. We can access a huge range of information and contact people from all around the world in under a second—all with a simple tap. The Internet of Things also allows us to connect everyday devices, such as lights and heaters in our homes, using the Internet.

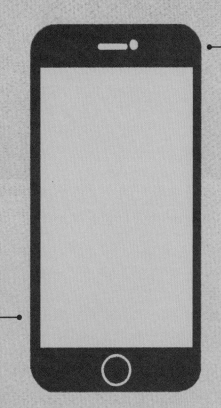

Around **3.4 billion** people owned a smartphone in 2016.

A single smartphone has more power than all the computers used to send Apollo 11 into space.

WEARABLE TECHNOLOGY LIKE SMART GLASSES AND WATCHES WILL BE MORE COMMON IN THE FUTURE.

BIOMEDICAL ENGINEERING

There is far more to engineering than creating buildings and vehicles. Biomedical engineers are making huge advances in the health and well-being industries, coming up with new ways to help people live longer and healthier lives. 3D printing has provided exciting new opportunities for biomedical engineers, as it is now easier and more affordable than ever to create complex prosthetic limbs. It may soon be possible to print hearts and other internal organs for transplant patients. This could potentially save thousands of lives.

You can 3D print in almost any material, including wood, metal, and even living tissue.

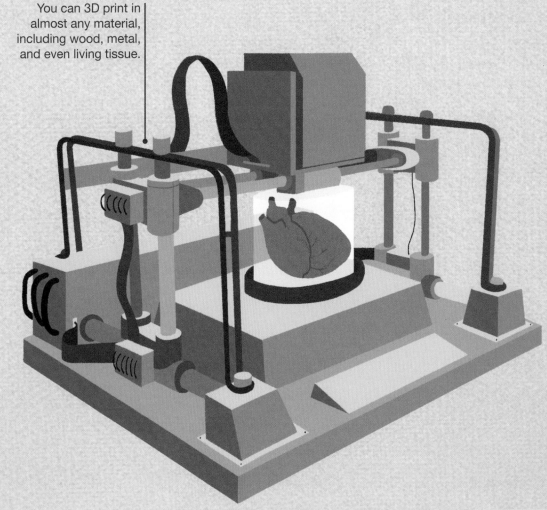

GLOSSARY

ALTITUDE
Height above sea level.

AQUEDUCT
A bridge that transports water over difficult terrain.

ARRAY
A group of objects, such as solar panels, that form a unit.

BORING MACHINE
A machine used to dig tunnels.

BREAKWATER
A barrier built to protect an area from high waves.

CANTILEVER
A projecting beam, fixed at one end, often used when building bridges.

COUNTERBALANCE
A weight used to balance another weight.

CURTAIN WALL
A light wall, often used in skyscrapers, that surrounds a building but does not support the roof.

CUT-AND-COVER
A tunnel-making method where a hole is dug and then covered over.

DIESEL-ELECTRIC ENGINE
A diesel engine that powers an electric generator, often used in trains.

DREDGE
To clear the bed of a river, lake, or ocean by scooping up mud, sand, and debris.

ERODE
To gradually wear away, often by water or weather.

FOUNDATION
The lowest part of a building, which must support the weight of the rest of the structure.

HYDROELECTRIC
Creating electricity using water.

KINETIC ENERGY
Energy created through movement.

LIQUEFACTION
The process of turning a solid or gas into a liquid.

MICROGRAVITY
Very weak gravity.

MONOLITH
A structure carved out of a single piece of rock.

MOTIF
A recurring image or design.

OBSIDIAN
A hard black volcanic rock.

ORBIT

The path taken by one object as it revolves around another.

OXIDATION

The chemical process in which iron reacts with oxygen, forming rust.

PAGODA

A tiered tower with multiple eaves traditional in parts of Asia.

PHOTON

A light particle.

PHOTOVOLTAIC

Creating electricity using light.

PLINTH

The base that a statue stands on.

PROSTHETIC

An artificial body part.

RESERVOIR

An artificial lake that supplies water to a community.

SARSEN

A type of sandstone boulder.

SCRAPPED

Removed from service and turned into scrap metal.

SHEET GLASS

Large panes of glass.

SOLAR

Relating to the sun.

SONIC BOOM

A loud, explosive sound created by an object traveling faster than the speed of sound.

TECTONIC PLATES

Massive slabs of rock that make up the earth's crust.

TUBE-IN-A-TUBE

A skyscraper building technique made popular by Fazlur Rahman Khan.

TUNED MASS DAMPER

A large device that helps to counterbalance buildings in earthquakes.

TURBINE

A machine that creates energy using a spinning wheel or rotor.

TYRANNY

Cruel or oppressive rule.

VENTILATION

The act of providing fresh air.

INDEX

ABOUT THE CREATORS

ABOUT THE AUTHOR

Colin Hynson worked at the Science Museum of London before becoming a children's and educational writer. He has written more than thirty nonfiction books for young people. He has also been a scriptwriter, appeared on radio and television, and written for the *Guardian*, the educational supplement of the *Times* (UK), *BBC History* magazine, and various computing magazines. He lives in Norwich, England.

ABOUT THE ILLUSTRATOR

Giulia Lombardo is a children's illustrator who studied entertainment design at the Nemo Academy of Digital Arts in Italy. She has illustrated many different subjects, but she especially loves to draw buildings, cities, and architecture. She works surrounded by cats, dogs, rabbits, and a chicken in her home in Florence, Italy.